This is the story of fifty years in which Britain has struggled to reconcile the past she could not forget with the future she could not avoid. It is the history of an attitude to history itself... Can Britain truly accept that her modern destiny was to be a European country?'

THIS BLESSED PLOT

HUGO YOUNG

BRITAIN AND EUROPE FROM CHURCHILL TO BLAIR

An insider's history of the biggest
story in post-war politics, told with wit and
authority by the leading political commentator
and bestselling author of *One of Us*

THIS BLESSED PLOT
Britain and Europe from Churchill to Blair

Available from early November

GRANTA 64, WINTER 1998

EDITOR *Ian Jack*
DEPUTY EDITOR *Liz Jobey*
MANAGING EDITOR *Karen Whitfield*
EDITORIAL ASSISTANT *Sophie Harrison*

CONTRIBUTING EDITORS *Neil Belton, Pete de Bolla, Frances Coady, Ursula Doyle, Will Hobson, Blake Morrison, Andrew O'Hagan, Robert Winder (Russia)*

FINANCE *Geoffrey Gordon*
ASSOCIATE PUBLISHER *Sally Lewis*
SALES *David Hooper*
PUBLICITY *Gail Lynch*
SUBSCRIPTIONS *John Kirkby, Darryl Wilks*
PUBLISHING ASSISTANT *Mark Williams*
TO ADVERTISE CONTACT *Jenny Shramenko* 0171 274 0600

PUBLISHER *Rea S. Hederman*

Granta, 2-3 Hanover Yard, Noel Road, London N1 8BE
Tel 0171 704 9776 Fax 0171 704 0474
e-mail for editorial: editorial@grantamag.co.uk

Granta US, 1755 Broadway, 5th Floor, New York, NY 10019-3780, USA
Website: www.granta.com

TO SUBSCRIBE call 0171 704 0470 or e-mail subs@grantamag.co.uk
A one-year subscription (four issues) costs £24.95 (UK), £32.95 (rest of Europe) and £39.95 (rest of the world).

Granta is printed in the United States of America. The paper used in this publication meets the minimum requirements of American National Standard for Information Sciences — Permanence of Paper for Printed Library Materials, ANSI Z39.48-1984. ∞

Granta is published by Granta Publications and distributed in the United Kingdom by Bloomsbury, 38 Soho Square, London W1V 5DF, and in the United States by Penguin Books USA Inc, 375 Hudson Street, New York, NY 10014, USA. This selection copyright © 1998 Granta Publications.

Design: The Senate
Front cover photograph: Magnum Photos; back cover: John Ranard

ISBN 0 903141 24 8

UNDERWORLD
'THE GREAT AMERICAN BOOK OF THE NINETIES'
Geoff Dyer, Sunday Telegraph
DON
DELILLO
DON'T LEAVE THE
CENTURY WITHOUT IT
ON SALE IN PAPERBACK
DECEMBER 18
PICADOR

GRANTA 64

Russia: the Wild East

THE METAPHYSICAL TOUCH

SYLVIA BROWNRIGG

An engrossing story of love between two people who have yet to meet...

'Brownrigg is a writer with a sophisticated and elegant feeling for words who is able to run far with the myriad potentialities of language'
GUARDIAN

'British fiction is stranger, and livelier, for her work'
TIMES LITERARY SUPPLEMENT

'Sylvia Brownrigg is... a true original'
THE TIMES

'A new imagination'
OBSERVER

GOLLANCZ
An imprint of Cassell plc

INTRODUCTION

Russia is the largest country in the world—a sixth of its land mass—with a record of upheaval, terror and bloodshed unparalleled in this century. First, the revolution of 1905, bloodily suppressed; then the revolution of 1917, bloodily won; then Stalinism, with millions killed in its forced migrations, exterminations and prison camps; and (concurrent with the last) invasion by Germany and a war in which upwards of twenty million Soviet citizens died. Finally, after decades of sacrifice which turn the Soviet Union into a military rival of the United States, acknowledgement that it has all been for nothing, that capitalism and liberal democracy have won; and with their victory comes the shredding of a state, an empire, a way of living and thinking—and pre-revolutionary levels of social inequity. To be a Russian old enough to have lived through most of this is to know extremes of hardship and disillusion that other people, at least in other industrialized nations (even Germany), can barely imagine. As Anatol Lieven writes in his new book on the recent Chechen war, *Chechnya: Tombstone of Russian Power*: 'To most of its inhabitants the Soviet Union was more than just a civilization, or a warped version of modernity. It was indeed a world, the only one they knew, and—according to its founders and mentors—the greatest of all worlds, the summit of human history, knowledge and achievement.'

'Reform' is the word that the West has attached, optimistically, to Russia's new condition, in which taxes and wages go unpaid, gross domestic product and life-expectancy decline, the rouble crashes and inflation (in 1998) runs at 200 per cent; where fear of the state and its laws has been replaced by corruption, crime and ruthless self-interest—'bandit capitalism'. These are, as Lieven writes, not so much unfortunate by-products of 'reform' as the phenomena at the very heart of it. If the Russian people were not so soured, confused and exhausted by their experience of ideology, one might be tempted to say that, once again, they looked ripe for revolution.

In literature, Russia has a great, perhaps the greatest, tradition of realism, which seems to have come to a temporary halt. Perhaps because reality itself is now so quicksilver and the truth about it no longer repressed, new Russian writers often favour satire and allegorical fantasy, forms which, when they lose their social context, can face a difficult crossing to other societies and languages. This issue of *Granta* contains an example that has made the crossing successfully: the piece by Victor Pelevin. It also includes, by contrast, a newly translated story by Andrei Platonov, who died in 1951 and most of whose work was banned until the last years of Soviet rule. Only in the past decade has he come to be recognized—but not widely enough—as one of the finest Russian writers of prose this century. His story, 'The River Potudan', is hypnotic in its quiet strength and sincerity; written of a time when it looked as though the future had been won. IJ

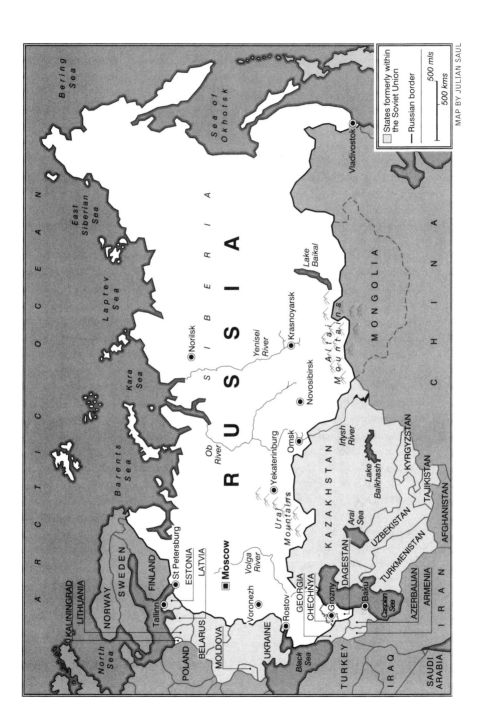

GRANTA

SIBERIA
Colin Thubron

Pilgrims bathe in the Velikaya River, Kirov

The faintly clownish name of Omsk raises light-hearted expectations. The city lies where the railway crosses the Irtysh River on a massive cantilever bridge, and you see the curve of the water under a line of stooping cranes as it heads out among sandy islets and meadows, touching the city with an illusion of peace. But beyond, the suburbs bristle with petrochemical plants, textile combines and oil refineries, and the pollution is so thick that driving at night has sometimes been forbidden. They sprawl for miles above the river. Marx Prospect, Lenin Square, Partisan Street: the veteran names follow one another in relentless procession.

Yet the city has a modest distinction. Whereas the Second World War razed many western Russian towns to the ground, here in Siberia, untouched, they often attain a formal grandeur or rustic exuberance, and seem older than they are. I wandered the streets in surprise. The municipal flower-beds were all in bloom, and fountains played between provincial ministries. Close above the river, nineteenth-century streets dipped and swung in icing-sugar façades of fawn and white. The air in the parks clattered with pop music. Clusters of mini-skirted girls paraded their irregular beauty, and children strolled with their parents in sleepy obedience; but their jeans and T-shirts were stamped with stars-and-stripes or Donald Duck. Every other pair of shoes or trousers sported a pirated Western logo. Fast-food restaurants had appeared, offering instant *pelmeni*—the Siberian ravioli—or anonymous steaks with stale mash, and a rash of small shops and kiosks had broken out, selling the same things.

Yet a feeling of boredom, or of waiting, pervaded everything. All style and music, the new paths to paradise, seemed synthetic, borrowed. Real life remained on hold. The pop songs had the scuttling vitality of shallow streams. The bus shelters and underpasses, stinking of urine, were rife with graffiti: POMPONIUS NAUTILUS—I LOVE YOU! AGATHA CHRISTIE! SEPULCHRE! THE PRODIGY! It took me some time to realize that these were pop groups; other graffiti accompanied them, sometimes scrawled in English, the lingua franca of youth. JIM MORRISON LIVES! NO!... I FUCKED THE BITCH!... COMMUNISTS ARE ALL BUGGERS... Then, in Russian, enigmatically: WHY TRAVEL WITH A CORPSE?... THE POINT OF LIFE IS TO PONDER THE CROSS ON YOUR GRAVE...

A pervasive frustration pronounced that freedom, once again, had proved illusory. Scarce jobs and high prices were the new slave-masters. The pavements were dotted with the new poor. Yet in this August sunlight I was touched by the traveller's confusion: the gulf between the inhabitant and the stranger. A little architectural charm, or a trick of the light, could turn other people's poverty to a bearable snapshot. The air was seductively still. Naked children were splashing in the polluted river.

I walked over the headland where the old fort had spread, but trees and terraces had blurred away the lines traced by its stockade, and only a stout, whitewashed gate remained. For four years Dostoevsky had languished here in a wooden prison, condemned to hard labour for activities in a naively revolutionary circle in St Petersburg. Sometimes he would gaze yearningly across the Irtysh at the nomad herdsmen, and would walk round the stockade every evening, counting off its stakes one by one as his sentence expired. He transmuted his life here into *The House of the Dead*, and it was here, among convicts who at first filled him with loathing but later with awe, that he experienced a half-mystical reconciliation with his own Russian people.

On the site of the vanished prison, fifty years later, rose a fantastical baroque theatre, painted white and green. Now it was showing *The Merry Wives of Windsor*, Alan Ayckbourn's *Season's Greetings* and Shelagh Delaney's *A Taste of Honey*. The only prison building to survive was the house of the governor, a purple-faced drunkard and sadist in Dostoevsky's day, who would have his prisoners flogged for any misdemeanour, or none. His home has been turned into a museum to the writer he hated.

A century after Dostoevsky's incarceration, Solzhenitsyn was escorted through Omsk on his way to a labour camp in Kazakhstan. He and his fellow prisoners were incarcerated in a vaulted stone dungeon whose single window opened from a deep shaft above them. He never forgot how they huddled together under a fifteen-watt bulb, while an elderly churchwarden sang to them, close to dying: how the old man's Adam's apple quivered as he stood beneath the mouth of the hopeless shaft, and his voice, trembling with death and feeling, floated out an old revolutionary song:

Though all's silent within,
It's a jail, not a graveyard—
Sentry, ah, sentry, beware!

The Pilgrims of Omsk

My hotel costs five dollars a night. The plaster falls in chunks from the walls of its corridors, and from the Stalinist mouldings of the ceiling. The night is close and humid. It is over 85°F. I lie on the bed and watch the full moon shining through a pattern of dainty flowers in the lace curtains. I cannot sleep. The sweat leaks from my chest and forehead. And this is Siberia.

Next morning, outside the big, unlovely cathedral, which in Stalin's day had been a cinema, I found a coachload of pilgrims setting off for a rural monastery. They welcomed me on board. The monastic foundations were only just being laid, they said, and they were going to attend the blessing of its waters. In 1987 an excavator at the site—near the state farm of Rechnoi—had unearthed a mass grave, and the place was revealed as a complex of labour camps, abandoned at Stalin's death. The inmates, mostly intelligentsia, had died of pneumonia and dysentery from working in the fields, and their graves still scattered its earth.

As our bus bowled through ramshackle villages, the pilgrims relayed the story with murmurs of motherly pity. They were elderly women for the most part, indestructible babushkas in flower-printed dresses and canvas shoes, whose gnarled hands were closed over prayer books and bead-strings, and whose headscarves enshrined faces of genial toughness. When a fresh-faced cantor began chanting a hymn in the front of the bus, their voices rose in answer one after another, like old memories, reedy and melodious from their heavy bodies, until the whole bus was filled with their singing.

We reached a birch grove on the Rechnoi farm. It was one of those ordinary rural spots whose particular darkness you would not guess. As the babushkas disembarked, still singing, the strains of other chanting echoed from a chapel beyond the trees. It was the first of four shrines which would one day mark the corners of an immense compound. Inside, a white-veiled choir was lilting the sad divisions of the Liturgy. As the pilgrims visited their favourite icons, a forest fire of votive candle-flame sprang up beneath the iconostasis, and two or three babushkas trembled to their knees.

In the south transept, still meshed in scaffolding, an unfinished fresco of the Deposition from the Cross loomed above us. It was almost complete; but the flesh tints were still missing, as if the artist were afraid to touch too closely on Divinity, and pots of pigment still lined the scaffold. So only the coloured garments of the disciples semaphored their grief, while their hands and features were empty silhouettes in the plaster: here a face uplifted in dismay, there a blank caress on the unpainted body of Christ, which remained a ghostly void, like something the onlookers had imagined.

Sometimes, whimsically, I felt as if this scene were echoed in the nave where I stood, where around the great silence left by God the worshippers lifted their heads and hands, crossed themselves, and wept a little.

From outside came the squeal of bulldozers in a distant field. They were smoothing the earth of the labour camps into monastery foundations. I strained to catch the sounds, but our singing drowned them in the sad decrescendos of the Russian rite. And out of the mouths of these ancient women—whose sins, I imagined, could barely exceed a little malicious gossip—rose the endless primal guilt, '*O Lord forgive us!*', over and over, as if from some deep recess in the national psyche, a need for helplessness.

The sanctuary curtains parted on an incense-clouded region inhabited by a very small priest. His hair shimmered down his head like a Restoration wig and melted into a droop of violet-clad shoulders. Occasionally, feebly, one of his arms swung a censer; in the stillness between responses its coals made a noise like suppressed laughter. As he intoned the prayers he constantly forgot or lost his place, until his chanting dithered into confused conversation, and three deacons in raspberry robes prompted his responses with slips of paper. He would stare at these through enormous spectacles stranded in his hair like the eyes of a bushbaby, and try again. But the cause of his panic was plain to see. Enthroned beside him, giant and motionless, sat Feodosy, Archbishop of Omsk.

Towards noon a procession unwound from the church and started across the pasturelands towards the unblessed waters. It moved with a shuffling, dislocated pomp. Behind its uplifted cross, whose gilded plaques wobbled unhinged, the Archbishop advanced in a blaze of turquoise and crimson, his globular crown webbed in jewels. He marked off each stride with the stab of a dragon-headed stave, and his chest shone with purple- and gold-embossed frontlets, and a clash of enamelled crosses. He looked huge. Beside him went the quaint, dishevelled celebrant, and behind tripped a huddle of young priests in mauve, and the trio of raspberry-silk deacons.

I fell in line with the pilgrims following. It was oddly comforting. An agnostic among believers, I felt close to them. I, too, wanted their waters blessed. I wanted that tormented earth quieted, the past acknowledged and shriven. I helped the old woman beside me carry her bottles. My feeling of hypocrisy, of masquerading in others' faith, evaporated. As I took her arm over the puddles and our procession stretched out over the wet grass, Russia's atheist past seemed no more than an overcast day in the long Orthodox summer, and the whole country appeared to be reverting automatically, painlessly, to its old nature. This wandering ceremonial, I felt, sprang not from an evangelical revolution but from a simple cultural relapse into the ancient personality of the motherland—the hierarchical, half-magic trust of its forefathers, the natural way to be.

I had already seen it everywhere. Every other market, airport or bus station was staked out by a babushka selling prints of icons and religious pamphlets, and nursing an offertory for the restoration of the local church or cathedral. Holy pictures dangled from the dashboards of taxis, decorated people's rooms. God had re-entered the vocabulary, the home, the gestures of beggars crossing themselves in the streets. Far away in Moscow the Church was growing fat on concessions to import tax-free alcohol and cigarettes; while here in Siberia, traditionally independent but conservative, this corrupting embrace of Church and State was paying (I imagined) for our monastery. But the cross wavered and glistened confidently among the birches. Authority, as always here, was salvation. It sold peace in place of thought, as if these people were not worthy of thought.

Yet after the Communist hiatus, what had God become? Was He not now very old? And hadn't He lost too many children? On a road beyond the trees a troop of young men and girls were watching us from their parked cars, without expression, as tourists look at something strange.

How had these devotees survived? For sixty years scarcely a church was open in Siberia; the priests had been dispossessed, exiled or shot. Even the oldest pilgrims trudging through these meadows could scarcely have remembered the Liturgy from childhood. How had they kept faith?

'We had icons in my home, hidden in the roof.' The young priest was pasty and shy, with absent eyes. He had joined the procession late. 'My father worked in the stone quarries of Kazakhstan, so we lived miles from anywhere. But parents pass these icons down to their children, you see, and my grandmother's family had kept theirs. That's how I came to God, through the icons, through my grandmother. Not suddenly, but out of the heart'—he touched his chest—'bit by bit. It's very simple. God calls you out.'

We reached a place where a silver pipe, propped on an old lorry tyre, was spilling warm water into a pool. A blond deacon like a Nordic Christ planted the processional cross on the far side, and the archbishop, the priests, the acolytes and pilgrims, the babushkas with their bags and bottles, a few war veterans and one mesmerized foreigner made a wavering crescent round the water's rim.

The unkempt celebrant, clutching a jewelled cross, was ordered to wade in. From time to time he glanced up pathetically at Archbishop Feodosy, who gave no signal for him to stop. Deeper and deeper he went, while his vestments fanned out over the surface, their mauve silk waterlogged to indigo, until he was spread below us like an outlandish bird over the pool. At last Feodosy lifted his finger. The priest floundered, stared up at us—or at the sky—in momentary despair, recovered his balance and went motionless. Then, with a ghostly frown, he traced a trembling cross beneath the water.

A deep, collective sigh seemed to escape the pilgrims. Again the cavalcade unfurled around the pool, while the archbishop, grasping a silver chalice, sprinkled the surface with its own water, and the wobbly cross led the way back towards the noise of the bulldozers.

But the babushkas stayed put. As the procession glimmered and died through the darkness of the trees, and the archbishop went safely out of sight, a new excitement brewed up. They began to peel off their thick stockings and fling away their shoes. They were ready. They tugged empty bottles (labelled Fanta or Coca-Cola) from their bags. Then they clambered and slid down the muddy banks and waded into the newly blessed water. At first they only scooped it from the shallows. It was mineral water, muddied and warm. They drank in deep gulps from their laced hands, and winched themselves back to stow the bottles on shore.

Then it all went to their heads. Six or seven old women flung off first their cardigans, then their kerchiefs and skirts until, at last, stripped down to flowery underpants and bras, they made headlong for the waters. All inhibition was lost. Their massive legs, welted in varicose veins, carried them juddering down the banks. Their thighs tapered to small, rather delicate feet. Little gold crosses were lost between their breasts. They plunged mountainously in. I stood above them in astonishment, wondering if I was meant to be here. But they were shouting and jubilant. They cradled the water in cupped hands and dashed it over their faces. Holiness had turned liquid, palpable. You could drink it, drown in it, bring it home like a bouquet for the sick.

Two of the boldest women—cheery, barrel-chested ancients—made for the gushing silver pipe and thrust their heads under it. They sloshed its torrent exultantly over one another, then submerged in it and drank it wholesale. They shouted at their friends still on land, until one or two of the younger women lifted their skirts and edged in. Bottle after bottle was filled and lugged to shore. But it was the young, not the old, who hesitated. The old were in high spirits. One of them shouted at me to join them, but I was caught between laughter and tears. These were women who had survived all the Stalin years, the deprivation, the institutional suffering, into a long widowhood and breadline pensions. Their exuberance struck me dumb. Perhaps, in this sacred and chaotic waterhole, the world seemed finally to make sense to them, and all this aching, weary flesh at last found absolution.

The procession, meanwhile, had reached the open fields where the bulldozers worked. All the way to the future cathedral, which would stand in the compound's heart, the tarred pipes lay ready alongside their trenches, and the channel was blessed. I caught up with the remaining pilgrims clustered in the big meadows, beside the ghost-cathedral. Here Feodosy, above the lonely swing of a censer, blessed the terrible site 'where nameless thousands had laboured and died', and we stared across fields lacquered in blue and white flowers while the incense vanished over them. Sometimes I wondered if the past were being laid too easily to sleep, forgotten. But the monastery would countermand this, said the shy priest. In future years people would ask: Why is it here? and recognize its building both as a cleansing and a memorial. This was being done for the dead.

The procession moved on. I fell behind with a puckish war veteran hobbling on a stick, and found myself wondering aloud again: why, why had this faith been resurrected out of nothing, as if a guillotined head had been stuck back on its body? Some vital artery had preserved it. And as I watched the pilgrims filtering back towards us from the pool, I thought: it was the women. 'Yes,' the soldierly old man answered. 'For me it was my mother. We lived in a remote region near Voronezh—not in a town at all, you understand, just a country village. No church for hundreds of miles. My mother was illiterate, but she remembered all the prayers from the old days, and taught me them.'

I tried to imagine his old face young, and found an impish boy there. A dust of hair was still brown over his scalp. He said: 'And in the war, when I was on the front, she prayed for me and I for her, secretly. She gave me one of these'—he pulled a miniature icon from his wallet. 'Marshal Zhukov kept one in his pocket all through the war—and so did other generals. And nobody knew it.'

He paused from the pain in his foot. Neither his icon nor his mother's prayers had saved him from a German sniper. The bullet had opened up a ten-inch wound, and now he had this trouble walking. 'We didn't have bullets like that in Russia, it was a type of shrapnel. When it hit me, it exploded and shattered the leg bones. Now I try to walk like this…or this…but nothing works.' He said: 'God must have been looking away.'

When we arrived back at the chapel we found a long table laden with salads and jams in the shade. The babushkas had returned. Their serried hands were ready beside their soup plates in two ranks of sun-cracked knuckles and broken nails. The archbishop, presiding at the head, commanded me to sit beside him—'We have a guest from England!' he boomed. 'We must make him welcome!'—and I stared down an avenue of scarfed and nodding heads, which turned to gaze at me as one, and murmured 'England... England...' Their cheeks bunched into smiles, and faltering lines of teeth parted in welcome.

Feodosy pounded the table with a bottle. 'This is for you!' he said. 'It's our monastery water! It cures everything!' He read off the label. 'Chronic colitis and enterocolitis! Liver ailments! All gastric problems! Cystitis! Non-cancerous stomach ulcers! Duodenal ulcers...'

The babushkas crossed themselves and commended me to God. They looked deeply respectable. Nobody would have guessed that half an hour before they had been ducking one another half-naked in a waterhole. Yet under the benches their bags bulged with bottles of holy water and they were sitting becalmed, almost smug, in the warmth of their success.

Around me at the table's head the priests had turned pallid in the desanctifying light. Stripped to simple soutanes, they fingered their cutlery nervously around the archbishop. On his far side the celebrant appeared to be defensively asleep. His beard, I noticed, was fringed with white but auburn at the roots, as if it had turned white after some shock and he was getting over it now. Only Feodosy still looked formidable. His black eyes and aquiline nose broke imperiously through the gush of grey hair and beard which swamped his pectoral crosses and lapped at his nape. He hammered out commands at the nuns who had appeared from nowhere to serve us, or shouted down the table. 'Brothers and sisters! Pass the mineral water round!... Sisters, bring on the *kasha*.' The vegetable soup was gone in a trice, and soon he was ramming the rice into his mouth with giant wedges of bread. 'And no water! Sisters...' I wondered if he had been promoted for his looks. A burst of jet-black eyebrows lent him the glamour of a converted Mephistopheles. Nobody dared ask him questions. He addressed me in explosions of German which I could rarely understand. 'The man who found the first mass grave here— this was the hand of God—it was the local Party Secretary! And now he's become a priest, yes! He's chaplain to a Cossack regiment in Omsk. Sisters! Where is the bread?...'

He ladled a dollop of strawberry jam on to my bowl of rice. It was like being back at school. 'And in the spring we'll start the building of the cathedral, yes, God is in this place of tragedy!'

I gestured out to the fields. 'Built on graves?'

'Yes, there are dead out there.' He turned sombre. 'And everywhere. The monastery will gather information on them, and the monks will pray for their souls.'

'And what will you do with so much space?'

'Do?' he bellowed. 'We'll plant it with roses! Nothing but roses!' The enamel crosses trembled on his paunch. 'An ocean of roses!'

All down the table the faces broke into smiles again, and stray wisps of hair shivered free of their headscarves. As the meal broke up, one of the women tapped my arm and held out a thin blue sash stamped with prayers. 'This is for you,' she said, 'to wear on your train.' Then she committed me to God, and went back among her friends.

I spread the sash in my hands and read: 'He shall give his angels charge over thee, to keep thee in all thy ways. They shall bear thee up in their hands…'

Yes, I thought, I would wear it as a belt. I must have grown thinner, because my trousers were loose. I knotted it round my waist.

A light intoxication, something welcome and unexpected (for we had drunk only water) descended on me out of the half-healed land. A priest was tolling a carillon of bells on a makeshift scaffold near the chapel, but softly (perhaps he was practising) as if to lay to rest the spirits, and the pilgrims, by twos and threes, were returning to the coach. I climbed in among them. For a moment I wanted to believe that everything was as they believed. I was thankful for their stubborn needs and passions. I sat stifled between two babushkas (there was a shortage of seats) and they began to sing. 'Sing! Sing!' they cried. I hitched up my sash: 'He shall cover thee with his feathers,' it went on, 'and under his wings shalt thou trust…' Yes, I thought, everything will get better. We will abrogate reason and love one another. Perhaps monastic water will turn us near-immortal. The past will forgive us, and the earth will bear roses…

Windy City

A land of interlaced earth and water, mutable, near-colourless—the sway of fescue grass above the swamps, the wrung-out platinum of winter wheat—spread from the train window to a thin sky. Halfway to Novosibirsk, the Baraba steppe was once a place of exiles and Tartar nomads, crossed by a string of Cossack forts. Now wild geese and coots flew from the marshes over a glint of lakes fringed by salinated soil. Here and there the old collectives were spread in long white barns, but they looked uninhabited. The villages, too, empty. Distance resolved them into the hamlets of Russian fairy tale, where the witch Baba Yaga might appear, or a formation of swan-princesses fly in.

In 400 miles we stopped only three times. I stared out to a faint, light horizon where the forest made charcoal lines. Occasionally a horseman watched his cattle, or a field of rapeseed broke into buttery flower. More often, for mile after mile, the late summer haze turned this into looking-glass country, refracting and confused. Its water-smeared earth wobbled against the sky. All matter looked temporary and dissoluble, all liquid so silted that it was halfway to being earth. Yet a farmer beside me said that the summer rains had been too few, and I noticed how low the rivers dawdled in their banks, and how the shrubs were already taking on the burnish of autumn.

We were following the line eastward of the Trakt post road, the precursor of the Trans-Siberian, laid in the 1760s from the Urals to the Pacific. In those days the bone-crunching journey—by horse-cart or sleigh—might take a year. When Chekhov embarked on his long tarantass ride towards Sakhalin, coughing up blood and sinking deep into depression, it was raining day and night, the rivers flooded, the ferries groping back and forth in howling wind, and ice floes on the move. Now, as we rumbled towards Novosibirsk, the largest city in Siberia, trains passed us every three minutes on the busiest freight line in the world, bringing coal from the Kuzbass basin to the smelting furnaces of the Urals.

You disembark at Siberia's biggest station, then taxi into the third most spacious city in Russia. Space is the sterile luxury of Novosibirsk. In summer it hangs in vacant stillness over the flattened boulevards. In winter it starts to move, and howls between the islanded buildings and across the squares. The city is a claustrophobe's dream. Its roads sweep emptily between miles of apartment blocks and Stalinist hulks moaning with prefabricated pilasters and cornices. As for the people, there are a million and a half of them, but they seem lost in space; they trickle along the pavements to work. You become one of them, reduced. The traffic seems sparse and far away, wandering over a delta of stone and tarmac.

Longing for intimacy, you avoid the 888-room Hotel Novosibirsk. But instead you find yourself in the void of Lenin Square, where the man himself stands in windswept defiance, his bronze coat flying out as if in a winter gale. Behind him the largest opera house in Russia, bulkier even than the Bolshoi, crouches like a square-headed tortoise under a dome of silver scales. To reach it you have to sprint two hundred yards across the traffic-sprinkled square. Then you are turned away. It is closed in August.

So you stand, a little ashamed of your indifference—for this, after all, is Siberia's industrial giant, its centre of heavy metallurgy and machine-tool manufacture, of international trade conferences and joint ventures—you stand on a traffic island christened by a gold-domed chapel: because here, it has been calculated, lies the geographical centre of Russia. You wait, as visitors wait in Times Square or Piccadilly Circus, expecting something to happen. But nothing does, of course. And you are alone. The streets reel away on either side. From the granite steps of the chapel you gaze miles down the main street at the shadow of a bridge over the Ob River, to where on the far bank glimmers a suburb of smokestacks and apartment blocks built in Khrushchev's time, now misted in smog. Here the Ob, the fourth longest river in the world, moves imperceptibly towards the Arctic—dropping only two inches a mile; soon it is filled with industrial waste and toxic oil, becoming so polluted that in winter it sometimes fails to freeze.

Space, in the end, may be all you remember of Novosibirsk. It is Siberia's gift. The vacancy of the land seems to infiltrate every town, or license it to sprawl. The apartment blocks carry on for mile after monotonous mile. Railway stations, whose tracks and sidings multiply ten or fourteen abreast, lie far from their town centres. And the rivers wind in enigmatically from nowhere like sky-coloured lakes, and curl out again to nowhere. The eye is met by eternal sameness. It begins to glaze.

Like the city outside, the restaurant is near-empty. A man and a woman sit alone four tables away. He is narrow-shouldered and rat-like, his eyes so small that they are almost snuffed out. She is a dyed blonde, running to fat. She is starting to weep. When she rubs her eyes, the mascara rings them quaintly, panda-like. I hear only snatches of their talk. Their right hands, each with a cigarette, are raised between them. 'Who with?... Have you understood?... Only too well... A lot, a terrible lot, too much...' Her thighs stir in their polka-dot dress. A two-man band—synthesizer and guitar—is playing from a gaudily lit rostrum. The woman lumbers to her feet and asks the guitarist to play something. Perhaps it is 'their' song. He starts up in the whining, nasal tones of Western pop singing.

> *Dancing in the streets of New Orleans*
> *Dancing cheek to cheek in New Orleans*

Her feet in their acrylic shoes start to tap unseen under the table. His do not. He turns away from the music and from her, smoking. Then her head slumps and her body gives a shudder. For the first time she stares at her bowl of undrunk soup instead of at him.

> *Dancing cheek to cheek in New Orleans*
> *Dancing with the Queen of New Orleans*

The salad and cold meat lie untouched in front of them. They smoke from the same box of cigarettes. To me they seem less present than the spaces around them, the distances that are too great.

Akademgorodok

In the mid-1950s, when the Soviet Union reached middle age, the rise of Khrushchev resurrected the old vision of a purpose-built city dedicated to science. This utopian artifice would solve the problems of pure knowledge; but it would also deploy its genius in the service of technology and economics, devoting itself in particular to the vast resources of Siberia, by which Russia would at last outstrip the West.

The embodiment of this awesome concept was planned twenty miles south of Novosibirsk in the Golden Valley by the Ob River. Building began in 1958, and within seven years 40,000 scientists, executives and their families had poured in to fifteen newly opened research academies. A garden city grew up in six micro-regions, with its own schools and supermarkets, an elite university, an artificial beach on the Ob reservoir, even ski runs illuminated at night.

Here in the taiga, far from the watchful Party apparatus in Moscow, a brief, intoxicating freedom sprang up. Akademgorodok became the brain of Russia. It attracted a host of young, sometimes maverick scientists, many from Siberia. It opened up fields of study previously forbidden. The Institutes of Nuclear Physics and Economics, of Hydrodynamics and Catalysis, shared the forest with academies devoted to geology, automation, thermophysics (for the tapping of volcanic energy beneath permafrost) and a Physiological Institute working on the adaptation of animals and plants to the Siberian climate. And at the centre of this cerebral spider's-web the Institute of Abstract Mathematics sat like a cool agony aunt, advising on the problems of all the rest. Informal communication between institutes was the touchstone of the place's founder, the mathematician Lavrentiev. There were breakthroughs in physics, biology and computer studies. For a few heady years it seemed as if the science-fiction city could fulfil its promise.

Then, with the fall of Khrushchev, ideological controls began to tighten. Science became yoked to industry and was commandeered to show direct economic returns. The heart went out of things. But in a sense the clampdown came too late. There were people working in Akademgorodok—the economist Aganbegyan, the sociologist Zaslavskaya—whose thought became seminal to perestroika. Yet ironically it was the chaotic results of Gorbachev's revolution that laid waste the powerhouse whose institutes I tramped for two days.

They rose in mixed styles, prefabricated, sometimes handsome, recessed among their trees along irregular avenues. There were now twenty-three of them, but the only map I found catered for visitors shopping in the town's handful of emporia. I scanned it in bewilderment. In Soviet times, I knew, maps were often falsified or full of blanks. This one featured greengrocers and shoe shops, even the smallest bakery and café. But the institutes had become ghosts. Not one was named. Were they too important to divulge, I wondered? Or were they just forgotten?

I wandered them in ignorance, staring at their name boards.

INSTITUTE OF SOLID-STATE CHEMISTRY... CYTOLOGY AND GENETICS... INSTITUTE OF CHEMICAL KINETICS... We barely shared a language. In between, woodland paths wound among silver birch and pine trees, their trunks intermingled like confused regiments. The earth sent up a damp fragrance. It was obscurely comforting. A few professors strolled between institutes, carrying shapeless bags and satchels, and fell pleasantly into conversation.

One of these chance meetings landed me unprepared in the Akademgorodok Praesidium. The professor who introduced me soon disappeared, and I was left in a passage outside the General Secretary's office, like a schoolboy waiting to be beaten. I thought I knew these interviews. From the far side of his desk a sterile apparatchik would tell me that all was well. The only signs of truth would be chance ones: damp wallpaper or indiscreet secretaries or the way the man's hands wrenched together. But I waited with suppressed hope. I wanted to know the outcome of several key Siberian projects, and sieved my brain for the Russian equivalent of 'nuclear reaction' or 'electric light stimulant', then fell into despondency. I wasn't even dressed right. I was still wearing my Orthodox prayer-belt, and one of my climbing boots had developed a foolish squeak.

When the General Secretary's door opened, my heart sank. He loomed big and surly behind his desk, in shirtsleeves. His features were obscure oases in the blank of his face: pin-prick eyes, a tiny, pouting mouth. I squeaked across the room to shake his hand. It was soft and wary. It motioned me to sit down.

Where could I tactfully begin? He wasn't going to help. He was gazing at me in passive suspicion. So I asked after the institute's recent successes.

He went on staring. All his answers came slowly, pronounced in the gravelly bass of authority. Progress had been made in the climatic adaptation of livestock, especially sheep, he said, and in a biochemical substance to stimulate the growth of wheat and rice... But he did not enlarge on this. I thought he looked faintly angry.

Then I hunted for projects safely past, and alighted on the perilous Soviet scheme for steering Siberian rivers away from the Arctic to irrigate Central Asia and replenish the Aral Sea. He said:

'It was a useless scheme, horrible. It would have been an ecological disaster for both Siberia and Kazakhstan. Our scientists here were categorically against it, and the project was scrapped.'

I shifted nervously (my boot squeaked back) in the face of his morose stillness. There had been a project, I continued, in which artificial daylight was used to increase fertility in minks, foxes, pigs… It had something to do with the relationship between the retina and the pituitary gland, I remembered, and sounded faintly repellent; but the General Secretary might approve.

He said: 'I only know they breed different coloured Arctic fox-furs now.' He tossed a batch of imagined stoles dismissively over his shoulder. 'Blue, navy blue, green. Any colour.'

But the remembered words of Soviet apologists, of Lavrentiev himself, were crowding back into my head. Some thirty years ago they promised that nuclear power would by now be centrally heating enormous tracts of Siberia and flooding Arctic towns with artificial sunlight. *'Dramatic changes in Siberia will astound the world, changes that will make Siberia ideally suitable for human habitation.'*

I said: 'There was an idea for melting permafrost by controlled nuclear power…'

The Secretary was unmoved.

'That was just an idea,' he said.

I felt grateful for this honesty. But the voices of the old enthusiasts went on clamouring in me. 'It was proposed to fire coal underground,' I continued, 'to feed hydroelectric stations from underground funnels.'

A cigarette waggled unlit between the Secretary's fingers. 'It didn't work. It was impossible.'

'Then what about the scheme for fuelling power stations with steam, using the Kamchatka volcanoes?'

He shrugged. 'I haven't even heard of it. And it doesn't fall within the province of this institution…' He was slumped deeper behind his desk, huge in the slope of his beer gut. His eyes were ice-pale. I imagined they had no pupils. I felt at sea. My jacket had fallen open on my prayer-belt, which guaranteed me immunity from pestilence and the cockatrice's den. I hid it with my arm. I was unsure what a cockatrice was, but the General Secretary might know. He continued to glare at me.

By now my questions, his answers, and the voices from the still-recent past seemed to be interlocked in a formal dance. I lit despairingly on an old success story. 'The hydrodynamic cannon...'

'*It slices off whole layers of hard earth,*' Lavrentiev had said, '*and opens coal deposits in a matter of hours.*'

'They were discontinued years ago,' answered the General Secretary. 'They couldn't really do the job. The principle is now used only to press matter, not cut it open. The cannon could only drill a small hole...'

We had reached a strange impasse. It was I who was believing in a future, it seemed, and he who was denying it. But I floated out a last fantasy, something I had childishly hoped to see. Twenty years ago plans were afoot for a whole Arctic town enjoying its own micro-climate. Named Udachny, 'Fortunate', it would either rise in a transparent pyramid or shelter beneath a glass dome or spread along a sealed web of avenues and gardens. It had been promised within ten years. (Lavrentiev: '*Siberia will become the science centre not only of the Soviet Union, but of the world.*')

I asked: 'Where is this town? Wasn't there a scheme?'

'There was a scheme,' said the General Secretary remorselessly. 'But there is no town.'

I went quiet, foolishly dispirited. The voices of the failed future mewed faintly, faded away. Suddenly the Secretary leaned forward. 'Look,' he growled. 'Look...' I had no idea what to expect. His face was heavy with anger. 'We have one overriding problem here. *Money.* We receive no money for new equipment, hardly enough for our salaries. There are people who haven't been paid for six months.' Then his anger overflowed. He was barking like a drill-sergeant. 'This year we requested funds for six or seven different programmes! And not one has been accepted by the government! Not one!'

I stared at him, astonished. I realized that all this time his bitterness had been directed not at me, but at Moscow. Far from being a passive mouthpiece for his masters, he was furious with them. 'I don't know what policy drives our government, or even if it has one! Science is now as cut off from the State as the Church used to be. As far as I can see everything's run by Mafia!'

He delved into a box and found me a book about the past achievements of Akademgorodok. It was richly illustrated with bursting corn-heads and fattened sheep. 'We used to accomplish things,' he said, as I got up to go. Then, as if a boil had been lanced, his anger evaporated. All his face's features, which had seemed numb or absent before, creased and wrinkled into sad life. How curious, I thought, bewildered. He was almost charming.

'The future?' he said. 'When we have a government that realizes no country can do without science, Akademgorodok will flourish again.'

He accompanied me to the Praesidium steps, perhaps reluctant to stay in his gaunt office. I started, too late, to like him. As I shook his hand I no longer sensed the brooding menace of the apparatchik; in his place was an ageing caretaker, dreaming of other times.

I walk along the Ob Sea with a young scientist from the Institute of Physics. This is not truly a sea but a giant reservoir, which sparkles tidelessly. And he is not quite a scientist (although he calls himself one) but a research student from the once-prestigious university. He is wondering what to do with his life. The sand under our feet is not naturally there either, but was imported—two and a half million cubic yards of it—to complete the town's amenities.

And now everything is in ruins, he says. 'The younger scientists are leaving in droves, mostly for business. In business you can earn five times the salary you're offered here. Others have emigrated to the States and Germany. All the bright ones have gone.'

Gone to the countries their parents feared, I thought. 'And you?'

A stammer surfaces in his speech, like some distress signal. 'I'll go too.'

'To work in science?'

'No. Most of us can't use our scientific expertise. We just want a decently paid job, and a future.'

Our feet drag in the sand. The enormous beach is dotted with sunbathers, and some women are walking their dogs along the shallows. He says: 'A few years ago, you know, when people left university, there was terrible competition to get into the institutes. But now they'll take anyone. They'll give you a flat, of course, but what's the point of that if you can hardly afford to eat?' The question is not quite rhetorical. He wants to be a scientist still. But he doesn't see how. 'Only the dim ones stay. They do laboratory work for a pittance. The equipment's getting old. And nobody's working properly.'

We stop by the water's edge. For miles it is fringed by a flotsam of logs, broken loose from their booms somewhere upriver. For a heady moment their resinous smell returns me to my childhood by a Canadian river, where the stray logs became the playthings of a small, naked boy, years before Akademgorodok was even conceived.

The student is saying without conviction, without love: 'I'll go into business.'

He was an only child. Reclusive, almost biblically innocent. During the war his mother had escaped with him from the siege of Leningrad; his father had been killed. I had been given his telephone number by chance, and when he clattered up in his institute's car—a professional perk—I had no idea what to expect.

Where did Sasha belong? Not with Russia's troubled present, I think, but with the dreamers who scatter its nineteenth-century novels. His work consumed him. Many evenings he toiled through the night in a big, bleak building called the Institute of Clinical and Experimental Medicine. Even now, during the August break, the receptionist acknowledged him with pert familiarity. He studied in the basement, in a chain of dim grottoes—their electricity had failed—poring over data on magnetic fields. Beside his desk stood a rusty stove and an exercise bike, and two or three machines loomed against the walls in a fretwork of tubes and wires. But there must have been electricity somewhere because a fridge wheezed in one corner, and after a while Sasha disappeared to make tea. I waited. I might have been in the den of some harmless wizard. The walls were hung with prints by the mystic painter Nikolai Roerich—grainy mountains inhabited by hermits or traversed by pilgrims.

We drank tepid tea in the dark. Sasha was fifty-six, but boyish, bursting with enthusiasm and trust. A pelmet of chestnut hair fell over his forehead and his eyes were brown and puppyish. He was sad that he could not measure my magnetic sensitivity on the Heath-Robinson machine beside us ('No electricity!'), but he hoped I would enter the hypomagnetic chamber next door. 'You've seen these photographs?' He pointed to a cabinet. 'Those detect energy flowing from a patient's fingertips after just three sessions in the chamber!'

I stared at them: they seemed to show a jellyfish haloed in hair. I said doubtfully: 'What diseases can it cure?'

'It treats epilepsy, but the subject needs to be very sensitive. It's also helped with nervous paralysis and cancer.'

'*Cancer?*'

'Well, it's helped in diagnosis.'

'But what does the chamber actually do?'

Even to myself I sounded peremptory, but Sasha was breathless with evangelism. 'The chamber almost eliminates the body's natural magnetic waves! They decrease by six hundred times! And this allows *other things* to happen—purer waves. Things we can't be sure about.' He was beaming his boy's smile. 'But before treatment we need to know your prenatal development in each of the weeks between conception and birth. The interplanetary magnetic field, phases of the moon and so on...' He stared at me as if I must have this data on me, perhaps in my passport.

'I'm afraid...'

But he rushed on: 'The field-structure of our organism is very dynamic. Sometimes it is closed, sometimes not. Recently, for instance, we had a conference in Martinique, and the people there were very open, very. Their magnetic sensitivity, when we tested them, was first-rate. People need to unlock, you see. To open up!'

I began to feel jittery. I stared down at myself, wondering if I would open up, but saw only a scruffy shirt and a prayer-belt. The magnetic waves to which I would be exposed owed much, it seemed, to the astrophysicist N. A. Kozyrev, who had set up telescopic mirrors to record starlight simultaneously from the past, present and future. Kozyrev was Sasha's god. The astronomer seems to have believed that the universe was awash with a unified time-energy, in which intellect, matter and cosmic forces were bundled up in some Hegelian process which fascinated Sasha but eluded me.

'It all depends on your responsiveness,' Sasha said, leading me to the next room. 'The machine opens up psychophysical recesses not normally explored.' We stood before two identical chambers: grey, open-mouthed tunnels for the patient to lie in. They resembled MRI scanners or huge, open-ended washing machines, but were utterly plain.

I said stupidly: 'There are two.'

'Yes, but one is a dummy,' he said. 'If you lie quietly in each, you will sense which is which.' He straightened the mattresses inside them. 'Of course there are some people who stay closed up. Yes. There are, I should say, cosmophiles and cosmophobes. But seventy per cent are sensitive to it. Some get a feeling of flying, others of being lifted out of themselves. It depends on your sensitivity.'

His trust invited mine. I was determined to be sensitive. I climbed into one of the tunnels, feeling like dirty washing, and lay down. 'Lie quietly,' he said. 'Meditate.' I tried to empty my mind, but instead found myself scanning the arc of ceiling above me for some tell-tale sign. Was this the dummy or the real one, I wondered? I thought I discerned a trickle of wiring under its plaster, but decided this was only a structural joint. I lay still. A mill-race of thoughts started up, subsided. I closed my eyes and concentrated only on the darkness under their lids, where an odd grey plasma was floating. The room was silent. My mind attempted a thought or two, then gave up. But I felt nothing. Nothing. After a while I stared down at the circle of light beyond my feet, hoping for some sensation, anything, but saw only Sasha's face peering in. 'Relax. Meditate for five minutes. I have to check my fax machine.'

I meditated. But no, this was the dummy machine, I realized. I simply wanted to go to sleep. So I climbed out and confronted its twin. They both looked makeshift and somehow unreal, like stage props. But as I crawled into the second chamber, I felt a tremor of unease. Now I would be passing (Sasha had said) from Einstein's space into Kozyrev's space. Living matter would enter an immaterial dimension. Hesitantly I lay down and gazed up. I imagined a white blank. A long time seemed to go by. I tried to float. Again, nothing.

Now I heard a steady, rhythmic whirring. For a moment I could not locate it, then realized it came not from my head, nor from the tunnel ceiling above me, but from the next-door room. I thought: Sasha is pumping something, a generator perhaps. He is trying to activate my tunnel. So at least I know I'm in the right one. I lay down and tried again. The whirring continued, but instead of flying I seemed to be sinking into a bored catalepsy. My next thought was: the Russian Academy of Sciences is actually paying for this stuff, has been paying for years...

After a few minutes, tiredly, I climbed out. Despite myself, an irritated sense of failure arose. I fought it off. I'm not cosmophobic, I thought grumpily, I'm just English. I scrutinized the chambers for any difference: a give-away trail of cables or an extra metal coat. But there was none. The rhythmic whirring still sounded next door. I peered in and discovered its source: Sasha was riding his exercise bike.

'How was it? How was it?' He jumped off, sweating and jubilant.

I hazarded a guess at which was the real machine, but got it wrong. 'Maybe I'm tired,' I said. 'I didn't feel anything.' I hated to disappoint him. Momentarily I wanted the world to be as he wished it, riddled with cosmic benevolence. 'At least I don't think I did...'

I had fallen plumb into the insensitive thirty per cent. But Sasha brushed this aside. 'Let me show you something else...' My statistic, I could tell, would be lost in his own certainty. He had a way of discounting failure, I sensed. His wife and son, he had mentioned, lived far away in Estonia—she had returned to the town of her childhood. Yet he shied away from the word 'separated'. They just were not together. He had sealed the subject with a hazy smile. Sadness made him afraid, perhaps.

'You know there are certain trajectories of extraordinary magnetic power...' He was burrowing among his files. 'Just look at these, from Stonehenge. I find these most interesting.'

On to my lap he spilled sheaves of paper covered with random sketches. They were the result of an arcane experiment. Here in Akademgorodok one of his colleagues had sat encased in a curved aluminium chamber called 'Kozyrev's Mirrors', constructed to heighten the transmission of his 'time-energy waves'. While he concentrated his mind on a selection of ancient Sumerian images, other participants—sitting among the monoliths of Stonehenge over 3,000 miles away—had attempted to receive and sketch his thought-pictures.

'Look, look,' said Sasha. 'This is remarkable.' He pointed to a Sumerian original, which resembled a pair of gnats, then he riffled through the sketches. I saw spirals, boats, dogs, phalli, suns, stick-men, flowers, stars. At last: 'There!' Someone in Stonehenge had come up with a hovering bird. 'You see? You see?' He was glittering with faith. Never mind that all the other sketches—page upon page—bore no relation to anything envisioned, or that the gnats and the bird only dimly corresponded. Sasha was smiling at them like a cherub. He scarcely needed proof. He already knew. For him they were joining mankind to the cosmos, earth to heaven.

Redemption

An old man sits in his dacha in the Golden Valley. These country homes are given only to the elite—he is an Academician—and all along the avenue their stucco façades rear from tangled gardens, until the road gives out against wooded hills. The Academician's sitting room is filled with kitsch: glass animals, sentimental pictures, statuettes of the Medici Venus, the Capitoline Venus, the Venus de Milo. But there are icons too, and tense, miniature landscapes painted by a Gulag prisoner. I wonder vaguely what these contradictions mean. Sasha, who has brought me here like a trophy, has gone silent. He listens to the Academician, his mentor, with hushed respect. So do the Academician's wife and middle-aged son. The whole house smells of a damp dog which is hurtling through the undergrowth outside.

For a while we sit nibbling *zakuski* snacks and drinking vodka. The Academician hands me his latest book, *Cosmic Consciousness of Humanity*. Then they toast my future Siberian travels ('It's dangerous now, you know,') and I begin to squirm in my traveller's disguise, because they want to convert me to their beliefs. Unnoticed I open the Academician's book and read: 'The total world human Intellect in its cosmoplanetary motion is neither derivative from, nor some procreation of, the social movement (social-cultural historic development). It is a peculiar cosmoplanetary phenomenon in the organization and motion of the Universe Living Matter in its earth-adapted manifestation…'

Fearing an attack of cosmophobia, I close it up, and now, impatient with the trivia of eating, of small talk, the Academician announces: 'We must go upstairs and discuss.'

Years of deference, I suppose, have wrecked him. An old pedagogy and a new evangelism smooth his thinking to unchallenged monologue. In the study where we sit—his son, Sasha, myself—his books are stacked in avenues from floor to ceiling, all nestled in dust. While his wife stays downstairs, washing up, he explains how man's spiritual and mental life is shot through by galactic waves, and I cannot decide if this idea is a vanity or humility (and the Academician does not take questions). He often lifts his finger as he advances point by point, and his message grows in urgency.

'We are at a crisis in the world's development. The West is powerless, blinded by money. It can't *see* anything. *It can't think new.* It is only Russia which can show the way. Point Three: she can do this precisely, and only, because everything has been taken from her, and she is open! Yes, open! This is the moment! We have just a brief chance—now! In a few years it will be too late. Now is the moment for classical thinking and cosmic thinking to converge. We must save the world—not only Russia!—and unleash new ways of thought!'

He speaks as if in an echo chamber, and the message which he finds so new is resonantly old. It rings through the works of the nineteenth-century Slavophils, who half-mystically enjoined the ancient values of the Russian soul. It is the vision of Dostoevsky, Herzen, Tolstoy. Yes, Russia will save the earth! Truth will rise through suffering! Europe—rational, individualist Europe—is benighted by affluence. Only impoverished Russia can touch the heart of things, and rescue mankind.

I start to lose the Academician's thread. He seems to be talking about experiments with cosmic waves in a Thracian sanctuary in Bulgaria, and in the Arctic Circle north of Dudinka where I will be going. He drops sweeping abstracts and magisterial generalizations. His audience is solemn, grateful. Stray concepts surface in English, sink again. 'Spatio-temporal waves... Point Six...distant-image interaction...' Then he says to me: 'When you sail down the Yenisei, if you go with an open mind, you'll discover a new Siberia! We conducted experiments in Dikson in the Arctic Circle, and you'll find the magnetic channels between there and here are very powerful.' He asks: 'You've heard of Yuri Mochanov?'

To my surprise, I have. He is a Russian archaeologist whose

excavations in the lower Lena have uncovered evidence of an ancient Siberian people. Controversially he has set the date of their stone tools at more than 2,000,000 BC, matching Leakey's Africans in the van of civilization. He still worked in the town of Yakutsk in East Siberia, where I meant to find him.

The Academician is fired up. 'A civilization at least as old as Africa's! So what does that do to Darwinism? Now the classic view is that man evolved out of Africa, then spread east and north into Asia. But the excavations of Mochanov and others prove something different. They prove that Intelligence emerged in several regions simultaneously—in Siberia, in Africa, in Central Asia. In fact Siberia was the first!'

It all fits beautifully, of course. Here in Siberia—the symbol and repository of Russia's otherness—civilization itself began. And here the cosmic flow, the great communion, will be reaffirmed. Not that the Academician repudiates science (although he lives in its ruins). In fact, his finger is raised again. 'I hold that cosmic influences accompanied by changes in the earth's magnetic field were responsible for a sudden maturation in men's brains at that time. These early civilizations were in tune with the cosmos, but due to various factors they could not, in the end, survive…' His hands return comfortably to his lap. 'Darwin, you understand, is nonsense.'

I sit opposite him, writhing with rebellion at first, then oddly sad. Sasha is glowing. But I see an old man in tracksuit trousers and threadbare socks, who has gone off the rails. Sometimes I feel that he is talking not to us, but to himself, and that he is very lonely. I imagine him the victim of that self-hypnosis which sustained the great illusion of Communism itself—where ideas and dreams hover delusively over the wasteland of fact.
□

Russia in the Age of Peter the Great

Lindsey Hughes

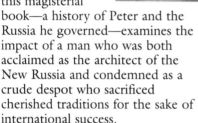

Drawing on previously unavailable sources, this magisterial book—a history of Peter and the Russia he governed—examines the impact of a man who was both acclaimed as the architect of the New Russia and condemned as a crude despot who sacrificed cherished traditions for the sake of international success.

"could hardly be bettered...will surely remain the standard account in English of this crucial and fascinating period."—Robin Buss, *Independent on Sunday*

640pp. 28 b/w illus. £25.00

Toward Another Shore

Russian Thinkers Between Necessity and Chance

Aileen M. Kelly

In this thought-provoking book, an internationally acclaimed scholar illuminates the insights of nineteenth- and twentieth-century Russian intellectuals into the social and political consequences of such seminal Western thinkers as Schopenhauer, Nietzsche and Darwin.

Russian Literature and Thought Series
448pp. £25.00

A Ved Mehta Reader

The Craft of the Essay

Ved Mehta

Unsurpassed as a prose stylist, Ved Mehta is an acknowledged master of the essay form. In this book—the first special collection of Mehta's outstanding writings—the distinguished author demonstrates a wide range of possibilities available to the narrative and descriptive writer today.

416pp. Cloth £28.00 Paper £12.50

Man from Babel

Eugene Jolas

Edited, annotated, and introduced by
Andreas Kramer and Rainer Rumold

This autobiography of Eugene Jolas is the story of a man who, as the editor of the expatriate American literary magazine *Transition*, was the first publisher of James Joyce's *Finnegan's Wake* and other signal works of the modernist period. Providing often comical and compelling details about such leading modernist figures as Joyce, Stein, Hemingway, Breton and Gide, the book enriches and challenges our view of international modernism and the historical avant-garde.

352pp. 16 b/w illus. £20.00

Yale University Press • 23 Pond Street • London NW3 2PN

Tel: 0171 431 4422 Fax: 0171 431 3755 e-mail: sales@yaleup.co.uk

GRANTA

SURVIVORS
Angus Macqueen

INTERVIEWS BY
ANGUS MACQUEEN AND
LIANA POMERANTSEVA

On my child's small globe of the world there is only one town marked on the north coast of Siberia: Nordwik. It stands a gentle twirl across from Moscow, and half an inch from the white expanse of the polar ice-cap. Nordwik, however, no longer exists. When I went in search of it for a BBC film on the Siberian prison camps, I found nothing but a couple of rusting hulks and a main street of deserted and decrepit wooden huts. Nobody has lived there for almost half a century. Its presence on a modern children's globe is a tribute to the American map-makers who, I suspect unknowingly, have preserved for our children the outline of Stalin's Gulag.

The most mysterious aspect of this is how the map-makers picked little Nordwik, and not its giant neighbour along the remote Arctic coast: Norilsk. Just half an inch to the west, and with large reserves of nickel, copper and platinum, Norilsk recently became one of the biggest prizes in the smash-and-grab that was Russia's privatization programme after the fall of Communism. Instead of feeding the Red Army's secret armaments industry, nickel is now being traded on the London metal exchange.

For years, I had looked at better maps than my son's, and dreamed of visiting this town in the middle of nowhere, this so-called St Petersburg of the north. But under the Soviets it was a closed city; its metals were mined for the military and its rockets pointed over the North Pole at the great enemy in the west. The only foreigners who went there went unwillingly, as part of the huge population of prisoners transported for weeks across Siberia by railway and then, during the two months of summer thaw, by barge up the Yenisei River. Through black, bitter winters, and mosquito-plagued summers, they were set to work mining in the permafrost.

Today Norilsk is just a commercial flight away from Moscow. It remains a secretive city, though. When I arrived, an Arctic snowstorm obscured its Stalinist splendours as effectively as any amount of old-style Soviet censorship. Many of these buildings are indeed reminiscent of St Petersburg (another city built by slaves). They are eloquent reminders that Stalin aimed not simply to exploit but also to colonize and develop Siberia. The GULAG (the acronym for the General Directorate of Camps), with its millions of prisoners, was at the forefront of his attempt to industrialize the country. The closure of the camps after Stalin's death in 1953 did not halt Norilsk's growth. Many thousands of the newly released prisoners, having nowhere (and no one) to return to, stayed. Thousands of other Soviets—non-prisoners—were attracted to the city by high wages and generous subsidies. Norilsk flourished on amnesia. Books and films commemorated the idealists who had braved the appalling conditions to create this miracle of Soviet industry. The nickel factory is still named after the first camp commandant, a man who shot prisoners in the back of the head at random.

With the end of Communism, the subsidies have dried up. The owner of the nickel, copper and platinum deposits is a Moscow bank and it has little interest in subsidizing people and amenities that it does not need. The Red Army no longer builds tanks, and the price of nickel has dropped threefold since the end of the Cold War. The town needs to shrink. Three hundred and fifty thousand people must, the economists say, become fifty thousand. It is an easy enough calculation, on paper. But what to do with the people? There are neither trains nor roads out of Norilsk. Many cannot afford the air fare out, which is the equivalent of six months' pension. It has become a town of poverty and unemployment, and in these conditions— freezing winters that last for ten months—poverty kills. Perhaps Norilsk, like Nordwik, is destined one day to be nothing more than a name on an out-of-date map. The interviews on the following pages record the memories and fears of the dispossessed. As one woman, the daughter of a prisoner, said: 'We have nowhere to go and nothing to go with. We are in a camp again.'   **AM**

Norilsk: as the prisoners of the Gulag remember it

Nikolai Abakhumov

Former deputy commander, Norilsk Garrison.

You know, Norilsk was a very nice town when I lived there. The houses were new and warm. It was a nice place to live. There was electricity. There were buses running along the streets, good buses. There were theatres. There were cinemas. There were restaurants. There was even a brewery. There were nice stores and a wonderful gymnasium. We, my future wife and I, would go dancing: we'd dance in that hall. There'd always be a regimental band, and we'd have a wonderful time, even though it was so cold. I'd dance in normal leather boots. It was minus forty, but I'd wear these boots instead of the felt boots they issued us to wear to work. On guard duty we'd wear these special felt boots with our big fur coats. Because it was so very cold. Even when you turned up your collar and turned down the ear flaps on your fur cap, so that only your eyes were visible, even then your eyes would be so cold that you'd close one until the one you were looking with froze, and then swap over.

That's how cold it was. Of course everyone suffered from it. And the wind. It was the same for us and the prisoners. And then in the summer everything turned into marshland. That's why it was so difficult to escape from Norilsk. Some people got out of the camps, but no one managed to reach the mainland—central Russia. First, there were the distances. It was 2,000 kilometres to the nearest big town, Krasnoyarsk. Around Norilsk there were tracks which would last a few kilometres before disappearing into the marshes. Nobody knew how far they stretched. People drowned. And then there were the mosquitoes. They would eat you alive. We used to find corpses eaten up by mosquitoes. Only the bones were left.

Maria Ivanova

From a peasant family near Leningrad, Maria Ivanova was left in German-occupied territory in the first months of the Second World War. She was shipped off to forced labour in Germany. Liberated by the Red Army, she was sentenced to ten years in the Gulag for 'betraying the motherland'. She was still only nineteen.

The pick you were given was usually too big for the hole, and for you. So you broke off the handle, and with this pick you had to break up the ten inches of permafrost that was the required work norm. We dug it all. All Norilsk was built by us. Now they drive piles into the permafrost but then the foundations for buildings had to be dug down by hand. And it was sometimes forty feet down. In the freezing cold and the polar night you could sometimes only see one star from the bottom of the hole—and how I used to look at that star. And I knew my mother was looking at this star. I had to see it at all costs. It helped me. When you work it is no longer so cold. The blood warms you, and the hope. The hope that you will survive, that was a double strength. The authorities would say you had, with 'your honest labour, to redeem your guilt before the motherland'. I was building for myself in my motherland and naturally I worked unsparingly. I also had to earn a full ration. It was a kilo of bread they gave, I think, for a completed norm. Or half a kilo—God, I don't remember now. At the end of the twelve hours they would winch you out of the hole, but only if you had completed your work. If you hadn't, you were just left there. When you had finished you would get into the bucket for the earth, like in a well, and they would pull you out. More than once the rope broke. And that was that. The bodies were left at the bottom. Norilsk is built on bones.

Gunner Krodders

Born in Latvia, Gunner Krodders was exiled with his family to the Norilsk region when the Soviet Union invaded his country in 1940. He watched his mother die of cold and hunger within weeks. But after Stalin died he remained in Norilsk, joined the Party and became a leading local journalist.

I read somewhere that people not only hated the Gulag but loved it too, loved it like you love your motherland. I think something like that happened to us former prisoners and exiles who have now become the strongest patriots of Norilsk. You see, after the camps closed, Norilsk developed into a unique world with its own intelligentsia and traditions, founded by the very people who were its victims. We were so proud of this city—the pearl of the Arctic. Now we are watching it die. OneximBank bought the mines and the factories, and Norilsk is a factory town. I can't blame the bank for the deterioration of life here, because the factory probably shouldn't have to support the social services and all the rest. But the state isn't doing it and the factory isn't doing it and no one knows what will happen: the houses are collapsing around us. And this is the Arctic. No one is doing anything. Because no one needs the town now: neither the state nor the factory. That's our tragedy. People think it strange that we, who were forcibly brought here, take such pride in it. But we built it. The prisoners were often educated people: engineers, managers, scientists and so on. They took pride in their work. And besides, the atmosphere was extraordinary. Nowadays people are stuck in their homes like mice in their holes, but in the Sixties and Seventies we would get together all the time. There was an orchestra and at least eight choirs in the city; there were clubs of every type—all free. Now you have to pay for everything and there is no money. So nothing is left. Life then was completely different. With Gorbachev's reforms we threw the baby out with the bathwater. We should have retained something. But instead we said: That's it! We threw everything out. Do I think Norilsk will exist in ten years? I doubt it. I doubt it. But it has to last another six or seven years because of the people. But what is to be done with us? Load us on a barge and sink it in the River Yenisei?

Alexei Loginov

A graduate of Leningrad's metallurgical university in the 1930s, Alexei Loginov became a senior manager in the huge metal industries of the Gulag. He was appointed director both of production and of the prison camps in Norilsk. In the 1950s he oversaw the closing of the camps. His ninetieth birthday was the occasion of a major celebration in the Norilsk factory.

Our country was preparing for war…but it is important to realize that this was not necessarily a war against the Germans. From the beginning we knew perfectly well that the outside world would never leave our Soviet revolution alone. Not only Stalin realized it—everyone, every ordinary communist, every ordinary person realized that we had not only to build, but to build in the full knowledge that soon we would be at war. It was inevitable—the Soviet Union would never be left in peace. So in my area, the search for all sources of raw materials, copper, nickel, aluminium and iron and so on, was incredibly intense. We had always known of the huge resources in Norilsk—but how to develop them up in the Arctic? So the whole venture was put in the hands of the NKVD, the Ministry of Internal Affairs. Who else could have done it? You know how many people had been arrested. And we needed tens of thousands up there. If we had sent civilians, we would first have had to build houses for them to live in. And how could civilians live there? With prisoners it is easy—all you need is a barrack, an oven with a chimney and they survive. And then maybe later somewhere to eat. In short, prisoners were, under the circumstances of that time, the only possible people you could use on such a large scale. If we had had time, we probably wouldn't have done it that way. We would have just gathered a few people and begun to build, first one house, then another. But then it was impossible. We were only beginning to build our country. So they had to bring, first of all, specialists who could build. And in the second place, people who could be used.

Andrei Lubchenko

As a fifteen-year-old boy in the Ukraine, Andrei Lubchenko escaped the occupying German forces and crossed back into Soviet territory. He was accused of spying, and sent to Norilsk for fifteen years.

There were people from all over the world in Norilsk: English, French, Germans, Chinese, Japanese. People from all the Baltic states, from Hungary, Austria, Bulgaria, from all the European countries, even Norway. We even had a Chinese welder. We just called him Vanya. Once I asked him: 'Where were you arrested? In China?' 'No,' he replied. 'We swam across the Amur River, between China and the Soviet Union—and they arrested us straight away.' I asked him why he'd done that. 'Well,' he said, 'we could see how beautiful it was on the other side of the Amur…the green and gold of the trees…and the steppes looked so beautiful! And everyone who crossed the river from our area never came back. We thought that this meant that life must be good over there, so we decided to cross. The minute we did we were arrested and charged under Article 58.6: espionage. Ten years.'

Khan

The port manager in Norilsk, Khan's Korean parents were among the mass deportations from the Far East in the 1930s.

What was it like to be the son of an 'enemy of the people'? It's hard to say. When I was a child I didn't feel it. I mean, I was already a third-former when Stalin died in 1953. And the way my school years were, I mean, practically of all the inhabitants, ninety per cent were enemies of the people. To tell one from another was almost impossible. When we grew up, when I finished school and went to university, by then times had changed. We did not remember it. I became a young communist and then a member of the Party. There was no other way.

Andrei Cheburkin

A soldier who marched in Red Square parades, Andrei Cheburkin had a number of jobs in the NKVD, the ministry of internal affairs. He started as a guard on the transport trains of prisoners, then worked in the camps before moving to Norilsk as a bureaucrat.

Life in Norilsk was better than anywhere else in the Soviet Union. In the first place, all the bosses had maids, prisoner maids. Then the food was amazing. There was all sorts of fish. You could go and catch it in the lakes. And if in the rest of the Union there were ration cards, here we lived virtually without cards. Meat. Butter. If you wanted champagne, you had to take a crab as well, there were so many. Caviar...barrels of the stuff lay around. I'm talking about the bosses, of course. I am not talking about the workers. But then the workers were all prisoners.

What was the pay like? The pay was good. In the mines...well, obviously if you were a civilian you wouldn't be doing the manual work, that would be for the prisoners. So say you were a brigadier, you'd get 6,000–8,000 roubles. In central Russia you would get no more than 1,200. I came to Norilsk as a work supervisor in a special directorate of the NKVD, which was looking for uranium. I was given a supervisor's salary—2,100 roubles I received from the first and then each six months I got a ten per cent rise, about five times more than they got in normal civilian life. You ask about the prisoners. Well, the prisoners were everywhere. They were brought to work under guard. And they worked. They did not bother anyone—they just worked and worked. They were slaves.

Norilsk: nickel factory, 1996

Yevgeny Kupchenko

The oldest inhabitant of Norilsk, Yevgeny Kupchenko was arrested in 1936 and charged with spying for Japan. At the time he was an illiterate peasant farmer. He was in one of the first groups to be sent up the Yenisei River to Norilsk. In the mid-Thirties the Soviet Union still openly talked of its revolutionary penal philosophy, which involved re-educating prisoners by introducing them to the joys of being a real 'worker'.

Re-education? Who would they be trying to re-educate? The prisoners? They taught with the cudgel, not with words. Why speak to prisoners? Do you think they said: 'We'll show you how to turn into good communists'? They never spoke to us. Nobody spoke to us. There was an 'education and cultural section' in every camp. But they just handled our letters. I had to give any letters to the 'education section' so they could read it and if they liked it, send it. But the idea that they would try to educate us—to do anything to cheer us up, to encourage us with explanations about how our country really needed metal and so on, never a single word. We were slaves. Animals. We were bullocks. It was like when, decades before, peasants in the Ukraine were used like oxen to plough the fields. And in these circumstances man becomes like an animal: silent and bowed. You never said a word. God preserve us from any conversations about the authorities or politics. Everywhere, even in the camps, there were informers. And you would be taken off to the security section and nobody would see you in your barrack again. Neither during my years in the camp, nor afterwards in the village, did I say a word. About anything that had happened. Not a single word. Even with my wife I never spoke about it. Now things are widely spoken about—that Brezhnev was a bad man and so on, but at that time a word about Stalin and that was that. If a newspaper with Stalin's portrait was found discarded somewhere on the ground, somebody had to be found and punished. And before the trial you'd be beaten until you were barely alive. And then: ten years in the camps.

Grigory Morozov

Grigory Morozov was a young conscript sent to Norilsk to guard the prisoners. He ended up marrying Julia, one of the 'fascists' (his word) he was sent to deal with.

We would enter a barrack, two guards and all those women… What women! Mainly young… My God! They were twenty-two or twenty-three years old. You know. So young… I wouldn't say that they were overly thin, you know—fat, some of them. Some were pretty, it was something. I would say 'Girls! What shall I search for in here?' And one of them would say: 'Come and search me, love.' She'd just take off her top. Deliberately, probably they were dressed like that… Well, she'd just strip off. 'What do you want to search for in here?' she'd say, 'We'd be better off…' I didn't know then that it was possible for women to rape a man to death. One time this girl said to me: 'Come on…' But I was still shy, and, as they say, I still had a conscience. I turned away and left.

All those women…our commanders told us not to mess with them. Once a group of women were to be transported elsewhere and replaced by men. And when the special transport detachment started to march the women off, I saw some guards running after them. Several men running after the women prisoners. Without their guns or anything. I shouted: 'What's going on? Why are you running after them?' They said: 'They're our girls.' The officers were shouting: 'What are you doing?' and all that. You know. 'Come on… Get back! Stop it!' And the soldiers were crying. You see, they had made friends there. They had got acquainted, everything. They were man and wife already. What a comedy.

Jadwiga Malewicz

As a teenager, Jadwiga Malewicz witnessed the Soviet invasion of her native Poland, then the German invasion. She also saw, through the long grass, the mass shooting of local Jews. When the Red Army returned in 1945 she was arrested for 'betraying the motherland'. Ten years in Norilsk.

I married my guard. The senior guard. I don't know quite how it happened. He was always looking at me. Staring. As he took us to work he would say: 'Brigade Leader, I'll marry you.' I'd reply: 'Nonsense, governor. You can't do that.' He said: 'We'll see.' Can you imagine? He guarded us for two years. And I never responded. I was very unfriendly. Three more years he waited for me. I kept turning my back on him. And so the day came. I returned to my barrack and saw the release form on my pillow. How it hurt. I thought: 'Where do I go?' They gave you this document, escorted you out and you had neither a room nor anything. Just go wherever you can. That's the way it was, you know. If I had had somewhere to go…but I couldn't leave. I sat on my bed, took off my Brigade Leader's armband and gave it to someone. I asked her not to tell my admiring guard that I had been released. But when I got to the gatehouse, there he was, waiting. I was carrying a small suitcase, made for me in celebration of my release. I had packed the little I had. He came up: 'Brigade Leader, let me carry it.' I said 'I'm not a team leader any more.' But I gave him my suitcase and, you know, dumb like a lamb, I followed him. He had made arrangements for a room. And when we got there, dear me! I saw the senior camp warder. He had rented a room with the woman who had for years been my warder. She said: 'You boasted you'd get that nice girl all the time. And here she is.' They started drinking. Pure spirit. That was all there was in those days. They drank. I couldn't drink at all: they gave me a gulp and I nearly suffocated. They were laughing. My 'man' staggered off to bed, and the woman said: 'Off to bed with you.' I said: 'Where to? What do you mean?' I sat at the table all night. But I ended up with him. What else could I do? I got used to it. I suffered torments for thirty years. In the end we got divorced. He left for his home village in central Russia and died there. He drank himself to death. I remained here alone.

Wanda Sosnor

When her husband, after a first period in the camps, was sent into permanent exile, Wanda decided to follow him. A rising star of Soviet opera, she organized prison concerts for the camp authorities.

We who worked there, both prisoners and exiles, even people like me who had gone by choice, were nothing but serfs. And I condemned myself to that. But I loved my husband. That is why I went. I wanted to help him. And who were my colleagues there? There was the conductor, the chief conductor of the Odessa Opera. There was a choreographer from the Kirov Ballet in Leningrad. There was Sevochka Topilin, Oistrakh's accompanist. Such people, such musicians! And I was there. Well, I was also, you know, a soloist in the theatre. They believed that I had real talent and a future. I could already have been working in the Kirov Theatre. I had been invited to audition for *The Queen of Spades*. I was in negotiations with the Bolshoi. Just as I was preparing to go to my husband, an invitation to sing there came through. But I had already decided.

After a rehearsal or a concert in the camp club, I would often listen to the radio quietly—to the music coming from Moscow, from so far away: a symphony or an opera. And I would stand there with tears running down my cheeks. But I always returned home with dry eyes. I could not show Sashenka [her husband] that it was hard for me, because it was hard enough for him as it was. I had to control myself. I was stronger, I was stronger because at least I could do something. I could theoretically go away somewhere. And he could not, he could not. His exile was, as they said, 'eternal'. ☐

Royal Festival Hall
Hayward Gallery
on the South Bank

Literature Highlights

Hot and Cold: Christmas Commissions
A shimmering, shivering end to the season as some of the hottest fiction writers read specially commissioned short stories inspired by the themes of 'hot' and 'cold'.

Wednesday 9 December
Voice Box 7.30pm
**Esther Freud,
Andrea Levy,
Duncan McLean &
Joseph O'Connor**

Tuesday 15 December
Purcell Room 7.30pm
**Diran Adebayo,
Lucy Ellman,
Tibor Fischer &
Julie Myerson**

Tuesday 26 January 1999
Purcell Room 7.30pm
Thomas Keneally whose *Schindler's Ark* won the Booker Prize and inspired the internationally acclaimed *Schindler's List,* talks about his latest book, *The Great Shame:* Eighty Years of Irish History.

Addressing the Century
100 YEARS OF ART & FASHION

8 October – 11 January From Matisse to Miyake, this exhibition brings alive the creative relationship between art and fashion through the century.

Next Exhibition
Patrick Caulfield
4 February - 11 April 1999

BOX OFFICE 0171 960 4242
For your FREE Literature and Hayward Bulletins with full details of all the above and more please call 0171 921 0734. OR SURF www.sbc.org.uk

Funded by
THE
ARTS
COUNCIL
OF ENGLAND

sbc

GRANTA

MOSCOW DYNAMO
Victor Pelevin

TRANSLATION BY ANDREW BROMFIELD

'Next station—"Dynamo".'
The voice from the loudspeaker snapped Serdyuk out of his reverie. The passenger sitting opposite, a weird-looking type with a round pock-marked face, dressed in a dirty padded kaftan and a turban streaked with splashes of green paint, caught Serdyuk's bleary eye, touched two fingers to his turban and said loudly:

'Heil Hitler!'

'Hitler heil,' Serdyuk replied politely and turned his gaze away.

He couldn't figure out who the man was or what he was doing riding on the metro, when an ugly mug like that should have been driving around in a BMW at least.

Serdyuk sighed, squinted down to his right and began reading the book which lay open on the knees of his neighbour. It was a thin tattered brochure wrapped in newsprint, with 'Japanese Militarism' scrawled on it in ballpoint pen. It was obviously some kind of semi-secret Soviet textbook: the paper was yellow with age and the typeface was peculiar, and the text had large numbers of Japanese words set in italics.

'The concept of social duty,' read Serdyuk, 'is interwoven for the Japanese with a sense of natural human duty in a way which generates the emotional energy of high drama. This duty is expressed in the concepts *on* and *giri* (derived from the hieroglyphs meaning "to prick" and "to weigh down" respectively) which are still very far from being historical curiosities. *On* is the "debt of gratitude" owed by a child to its parents, a vassal to his suzerain, a citizen to the state. *Giri* is "obligation and responsibility", which requires that each individual act in accordance with his station and position in society. It is also obligation in relation to one's own self, the preservation of the honour and dignity of one's own person, of one's name. Duty consists in being prepared to sacrifice oneself in the name of *on* and *giri*, which define a specific code of social, professional and human behaviour.'

His neighbour, apparently noticing Serdyuk reading his book, lifted it closer to his face, half closing it for good measure so that the text was completely hidden. Serdyuk shut his eyes. That's why they're able to live like normal human beings, he thought, because they never forget about their duty. They don't spend all their time getting pissed like folks here.

It's not really possible to say what exactly went on in his head over the next few minutes, but when the train stopped at Pushkinskaya station and Serdyuk emerged from the carriage, his soul had become filled with the fixed desire to have a drink—in fact, to take an entire skinful. Initially the desire was acknowledged merely as a vague melancholy, and only assumed its true form when Serdyuk found himself face to face with a long rank of armour-plated kiosks, from which identical pairs of Caucasian eyes surveyed enemy territory through narrow observation slits.

Deciding on what exactly he wanted proved more difficult. There was a wide but fairly second-rate selection—more like an election than a piss-up, he thought. He hesitated for a long time, until he finally spotted a bottle of port wine bearing the name 'Livadia' in one of the glass windows.

Serdyuk's first sight of the bottle brought back memories of a morning in his youth; a secluded corner, stacked high with crates, in the yard of the institute where he studied, the sun on the yellow leaves and a group of laughing students handing round a bottle of that same port wine. He also recalled that to reach that secluded spot, secure from observation on all sides, you had to slip between some rusty railings, usually messing up your jacket in the process. But the most important thing in all this wasn't the port wine or the railings; it was the pang of sadness which was triggered in his heart—the memory of all the limitless opportunities and endless highways in the world that had once stretched away from the corner of that yard.

This memory was rapidly followed by the unbearable thought that it wasn't the world itself that had changed since those old days, it was just that he couldn't see it with the same eyes any more. Still, if he couldn't view the world through the same eyes, he might at least glimpse it through the same glass, darkly. Thrusting his money through the embrasure of the kiosk, Serdyuk scooped up the green grenade that popped out through the same opening. He crossed the street, picked his way carefully between the puddles that reflected the sky of a late spring afternoon, sat down on a bench in the square opposite the figure of Pushkin and pulled the plastic stopper out of the bottle with his teeth. The port wine still tasted exactly as it had always done—one more proof that reform had not really touched the basic foundations of Russian life, but merely swept like a hurricane across its surface.

He polished off the bottle in a few long gulps, then tossed it into the bushes behind the low granite kerb; an intelligent-looking old woman who had been pretending to read a newspaper went after it straight away. Serdyuk slumped back against the bench.

The high hit him a few minutes later. The world was changed, and quite noticeably—it had stopped feeling hostile, and the people walking past him were gradually transformed from disciples of global evil into its victims. After another minute or two something happened to global evil itself—it either disappeared or simply stopped being important. The intoxication mounted to its blissful zenith, lingered there for a few brief seconds, before the usual ballast of drunken thoughts dragged him back down to reality.

Three schoolboys walked past Serdyuk. He could hear them repeating 'You gotta problem?' as they receded in the direction of an amphibious Japanese jeep with a bit hoist on its snout which was parked at the edge of the pavement. Jutting above the jeep on the other side of Tverskaya Street he could see the McDonald's sign, like the yellow merlon of some invisible fortress wall. 'The American Future,' Serdyuk thought, and then remembered the book he'd read on the metro.

'The Japanese,' Serdyuk said to himself, 'now there's a great nation! Just think—they've had two atom bombs dropped on them, they've had their islands taken away, but they've survived... Why is it nobody here can see anything but America? What the hell good is America to us? It's Japan we should be following—we're neighbours, aren't we? It's the will of God. And they need to be friends with us too—between the two of us we'd polish off your America soon enough...with its atom bombs and asset managers...'

Somehow these thoughts developed into a decision to go for another bottle. Serdyuk considered what to buy. He didn't fancy more port wine. He fancied something simple and straightforward and limitless, like the sea in the 'Travellers' Club' programme on television, or the field of wheat on the share certificate he'd received in exchange for his privatization voucher. He decided to get some Dutch spirit.

He went back to the kiosk, and then to the hamburger joint, and then back to the same bench. He opened the bottle, poured out half a plastic cupful, drank it, then gulped at the air with his scorched mouth as he tore open the newspaper he'd wrapped around his hamburger. On the newspaper there was a strange symbol, a red flower with asymmetrical petals set inside an oval. There was a notice below the emblem: 'The Moscow branch of the Japanese firm Taira Incorporated is interviewing potential employees. Knowledge of English and computer skills essential.'

Serdyuk cocked his head sideways. For a moment he thought he'd seen a second notice printed beside the first one, decorated with a similar emblem. But when he took a closer look, he realized that right next to the flower, inside its oval border, there was a ring of onion and a bloody streak of ketchup. Serdyuk noted with satisfaction that the various levels of reality were beginning to merge into each other. He carefully tore the notice out of the newspaper, licked a drop of ketchup off it, folded it in two and stuck it in his pocket. Everything after that went as usual.

He was woken by a sick feeling and the grey light of morning. The major irritant, of course, was the light—as always, it seemed to have been mixed with chlorine in order to disinfect it. Looking around, Serdyuk realized he was at home, and apparently he'd had visitors the evening before—just who, he couldn't remember. He struggled up from the floor, took off his mud-streaked jacket and cap, went out into the corridor and hung them on a hook. Then he had the comforting thought that there might be some beer in the fridge—it wasn't impossible. But when he was only a few feet from the fridge, the phone on the wall began to ring. Serdyuk took the receiver off the hook and tried to say 'hello', but the very effort of speaking was so painful that instead he gave out a croak that sounded something like 'Oh-aye-aye'.

'*Okhae dzeimas,*' the receiver echoed cheerfully. 'Mister Serdyuk?'

'Yes,' said Serdyuk.

'Hello. My name is Oda Nobunaga and I had a conversation with you yesterday evening. More precisely, last night. You were kind enough to give me a call.'

'Yes,' said Serdyuk, clutching at his head with his free hand.

'I have discussed your proposal with Mr Esitsune Kawabata, and he is prepared to receive you today at three o'clock for purposes of an interview.'

Serdyuk didn't recognize the voice in the receiver. He could tell straight away it was that of a foreigner—although he couldn't hear any accent, the person talking to him made pauses, as though he was running through his vocabulary searching for the right word.

'Much obliged,' said Serdyuk. 'But what proposal's that?'

'The one you made yesterday. Or today, to be precise.'

'Aha!' said Serdyuk, 'A-a-ha!'

'Write down the address,' said Oda Nobunaga.

'Hang on,' said Serdyuk, 'just a moment. I'll get a pen.'

'But why do you not have a notepad and a pen by the telephone?' Nobunaga asked, with obvious irritation in his voice. 'A man of business should do so.'

'I'm writing now,' Serdyuk said.

'Nagornaya metro station, the exit on the right. There will be an iron fence facing you and a house, with an entrance to the yard. The precise address is Pyatikhlebny Lane, house number five. There will be a... What is it now... A plaque.'

'Thank you.'

'That is all from me. *Sayonara*, as they say,' said Nobunaga and hung up.

There was no beer in the fridge.

Emerging from Nagornaya metro station long before the appointed time, Serdyuk immediately saw a fence covered with battered, peeling tinplate, but he didn't believe it could be the same one mentioned by Mr Nobunaga—it was somehow too plain and too dirty. He walked around for a while, stopping the rare passers-by and asking where Pyatikhlebny Lane was. This was something none of them seemed to know, or wanted to tell him—in any case, they were mostly old women in dark clothes plodding slowly towards some mysterious destination.

It was a wild place, like the overgrown ruins of a blitzed industrial zone. This was not one of the areas where serious foreign companies opened their offices, and Serdyuk decided this must be some two-bit firm staffed by Japanese who had failed to adjust fully to the demands of the changing world (for some reason he thought of the peasants from the film *The Seven Samurai*). It was clear now why they'd taken such an interest in his drunken phone-call, and Serdyuk even felt a surge of fellow-feeling for these slightly dull-witted foreigners who, just like him, had not been able to find themselves a comfortable niche in life—and the doubt that had been nagging him all the way there, the thought that he really should have had a shave, quite simply disappeared.

Mr Nobunaga's direction that 'there will be a house' could have applied to several dozen buildings. Serdyuk decided for no particular reason that the one he was looking for was a grey eight-storey building with a glass-fronted delicatessen on the ground floor. Remarkably enough, he spotted a brass oblong on the wall with the inscription 'Taira Trading House' and a tiny bell-push, almost invisible against the uneven surface of the wall. About a yard away from the plaque a crude iron door hung on immense green-painted hinges. Serdyuk looked around in consternation—apart from the door, the only other thing the plaque could possibly relate to was a cast-iron manhole cover in the asphalt. He waited until his watch showed two minutes to three and rang the bell.

The door opened immediately. Standing behind it was the inevitable security guard in camouflage gear, holding a rubber truncheon. Serdyuk nodded to him and opened his mouth to explain the reason for his visit—but then stopped.

Beyond the door he could see a small hallway with a desk, a telephone and a chair, and on the wall of the hallway was a large mural, showing a corridor extending into infinity. Looking more closely, Serdyuk realized it wasn't a mural at all; it was a genuine corridor which began on the other side of a glass door. This corridor was strange: there were lanterns hanging on its walls—he could see flames flickering through their rice-paper shades—and the floor was covered by a thick layer of yellow sand across which narrow bamboo mats had been laid to form a kind of runner. The same emblem he had seen in the newspaper was drawn in bright red paint on the lanterns—a flower with four diamond-shaped petals, the side-petals longer than the others, enclosed in an oval. The corridor did not actually run off into infinity as he'd thought; it simply curved smoothly to the right so that its end was hidden from sight.

'Whatyer want?' said the security guard, breaking the silence.

'I've a meeting with Mr Kawabata,' said Serdyuk, pulling himself together, 'at three o'clock.'

'Ah. Come inside then, quick. They don't like it when the door's left open for long.'

Serdyuk stepped inside and the guard closed the door and locked it with what looked like a massive valve-wheel.

'Take your shoes off, please,' he said. 'The *geta* are over there.'

'The what?' asked Serdyuk.

'The *geta*. What they use for slippers. They don't wear any other shoes inside. That's a strict rule.'

Serdyuk saw several pairs of wooden shoes lying on the floor. They looked clumsy and uncomfortable, with a strap that had to be inserted between the big and second toe so that you could wear them only in bare feet. Just for a second he thought the security guard was joking, but then he noticed several pairs of shiny black shoes standing in the corner with socks protruding from them. He sat down on a low bench and removed his shoes. When he stood up he noticed that the *geta* had made him three or four inches taller.

'Can I go in now?' he asked.

'Go ahead. Take a lantern and go straight down the corridor. Room number three.'

'Why the lantern?' Serdyuk asked in amazement.

'That's the rule here,' said the security guard, taking one of the lanterns down from the wall and holding it out to Serdyuk. 'You don't wear a tie to keep you warm, do you?'

Serdyuk, who had knotted a tie round his neck that morning for the first time in many years, found this argument quite convincing.

'Room number three,' repeated the security guard, 'but the numbers are in Japanese. It's the one with three strokes one above the other. You know, like the trigram for "sky".'

'Aha,' said Serdyuk, 'I'm with you.'

'And whatever you do, don't knock. Just let them know you're outside—try clearing your throat, or say a few words. Then wait for them to tell you what to do.'

Serdyuk set off, lifting his feet high in the air like a stork and holding the lantern at arm's length. Around the smooth bend he found a small dimly lit hall with black beams running across the ceiling. At first Serdyuk couldn't see any doors there, but then he realized that the tall wall-panels were doors that slid sideways. There was a sheet of paper hanging on one of the panels. Serdyuk held his lantern close to it and when he saw the three lines drawn in black ink, he knew that this must be room number three.

He could hear music playing quietly behind the door. It was some obscure stringed instrument: the timbre was unusual, and the slow melody, built upon strange and—as it seemed to Serdyuk— ancient harmonies, was sad and plaintive. He cleared his throat. There was no response from beyond the wall. He cleared his throat again, louder this time, and thought that if he had to do it again he would probably puke.

'Come in,' said a voice behind the door.

Serdyuk slid the partition to the left and saw a room with dark bamboo mats on the floor. Sitting on a number of cushions scattered in the corner with his legs folded under him was a barefoot man in a dark suit. He was playing an odd-looking instrument like a long lute with a small soundbox, and he took absolutely no notice of Serdyuk's appearance. His face could hardly have been called mongoloid, though you could say there was something southern about it—Serdyuk's thoughts on this point followed a highly specific route as he recalled a trip he'd made to Rostov-on-Don the year before. Standing on the floor of the room was a small electric cooker with a single ring supporting a large saucepan, and a black, streamlined fax machine with a lead that disappeared into a hole in the wall. Serdyuk went in, put down his lantern on the floor and closed the door behind him.

The man in the suit gave a final touch to a string and raised his puffy red eyes in a gesture of farewell to the note as it departed this world for ever, before carefully laying his instrument on the floor. His movements were very slow and economical, as though he was afraid a clumsy or abrupt gesture might offend someone who was present in the room but invisible to Serdyuk. Taking a handkerchief subscribe . . .

GRANTA

SAVE UP TO 30%

© PHOTONICA

... and get a **serious** discount.

Subscribe to Granta and you will **save at least £7** and **up to £28** on the bookshop price—and get Granta delivered to your home. See the prices on the order form below. You will get four fat issues a year of the most compelling new fiction, memoir, reportage, argument and photography that Granta can commission, inspire or find.

So why not treat yourself now? (Or treat a friend? A subscription to Granta makes a great gift.)

GRANTA

'Essential.' Observer
'Indispensable.' Glasgow Herald
'Remarkable.' Scotland on Sunday
'Wonderful.' The Times

Your details

Name _____

Address _____

_____

_____ Postcode _____

○ I'd like to subscribe for myself, for:
   ○ 1 year (4 issues) at £24.95 (22% off)
   ○ 2 years (8 issues) at £46.50 (27% off)
   ○ 3 years (12 issues) at £67.00 (30% off)
starting with issue number _____

Details for a gift subscription

○ I'd like to give a subscription to the person below, starting with issue number _____ for:
   ○ 1 year ○ 2 years ○ 3 years.
   (My name and address are on the left.)

Name _____

Address _____

_____

_____ Postcode _____

TOTAL* £ _____ by ○ sterling cheque (to 'Granta') ○ Visa, Mastercard/Access, AmEx

card no /__/__/__/__/__/__/__/__/__/__/__/__/__/__/__/__/ expires /__/__/__/__/

signature _____

98L5S64B

*Postage. The prices above include UK postage. Please add £8 per year for the rest of Europe; £15 per year for overseas.

○ Please tick here if you would prefer not to receive occasional promotional literature from other compatible organizations.

Return (free if in the UK) to: Granta, Freepost, 2/3 Hanover Yard, Noel Rd, London N1 8BE, UK. Or phone/fax your order:
   UK: FreeCall 0500 004 033 (phone & fax)
   Outside the UK: Tel 44 171 704 0470
                     Fax 44 171 704 0474

from his breast pocket, he wiped the tears from his eyes and turned towards his visitor. They looked at each other for a while.

'Hello. My name is Serdyuk.'

'Kawabata,' said the man.

He sprang to his feet, walked briskly over to Serdyuk and took him by the hand. His palm was cold and dry.

'Please,' he said, pulling Serdyuk over to the scattered cushions, 'sit down. Please, sit down.'

Serdyuk sat down.

'I...' he began, but Kawabata interrupted him:

'I don't want to hear a word. In Japan we have a very ancient tradition which says that if a person enters your house with a lantern in his hand and *geta* on his feet, it means that it is dark outside and the weather is bad, and the very first thing you must do is pour him some warm *sake*.'

With these words Kawabata fished out a fat bottle with a short neck from the saucepan. It was sealed with a watertight stopper and had a long thread tied to its neck which Kawabata used to extract it. Two small porcelain glasses appeared with indecent drawings on them. They depicted beautiful women with unnaturally high arched eyebrows giving themselves in intricately contrived poses to serious-looking men wearing small blue caps. Kawabata filled the glasses to the brim.

'Please,' he said, and held one of the glasses out to Serdyuk.

Serdyuk tipped the contents into his mouth. The liquid reminded him most of all of vodka diluted with rice water. Worse still, it was hot—perhaps that was the reason he puked straight on to the floormats as soon as he swallowed it. The feeling of shame and self-loathing that overwhelmed him was so powerful that he just covered his face with his hands.

'Oh,' said Kawabata politely, 'there must be a real storm outside.' He clapped his hands.

Serdyuk half opened his eyes. Two girls had appeared in the room dressed in a manner very similar to the women shown on the glasses. They even had the same high eyebrows—Serdyuk took a closer look and realized they were drawn on their foreheads with ink. The resemblance was so complete that Serdyuk's thoughts were only restrained by the shame he had felt a few seconds earlier. The girls quickly rolled up the soiled mats, laid out fresh ones and left the room—not by the door that Serdyuk had used, but by a second wall panel that moved sideways.

'Please,' said Kawabata.

Serdyuk raised his eyes. The Japanese was holding out another glass of *sake*. Serdyuk gave a pitiful smile and shrugged.

'This time,' said Kawabata, 'everything will be fine.'

Serdyuk drank it. And this time the effect really was quite different—the *sake* went down very smoothly and a healing warmth spread through his body.

'You know what the trouble is,' he said, 'Yesterday...'

'First another one,' said Kawabata.

The fax machine on the floor jangled and a sheet of paper thickly covered with hieroglyphics came slithering out. Kawabata waited for the paper to stop moving, then tore the sheet out of the machine and became engrossed in studying it, completely forgetting about Serdyuk.

Serdyuk examined his surroundings. The walls of the room were covered with identical wooden panels, and now that the *sake* had neutralized the consequences of yesterday's bout of nostalgia, each of them had assumed the appearance of a door leading into the unknown. But then one of the panels, which had a printed engraving hanging on it, was quite clearly not a door.

Like everything else in Mr Kawabata's office, the print was strange. It consisted of an immense sheet of paper, in the centre of which a picture seemed to emerge out of a mass of carelessly applied yet precisely positioned lines. It showed a naked man (his figure was extremely stylized, but it was clear that he was a man from the realistically depicted sexual organ), standing on the edge of a precipice. Several weights of various sizes hung around his neck, and he had a sword in each hand; his eyes were blindfolded with a white cloth, and the edge of the precipice was directly under his feet. There were a few other minor details—the sun setting into a bank of mist, birds in the sky and the roof of a pagoda in the distance—but despite these romantic digressions, the main sensation it aroused in Serdyuk's soul was one of hopelessness.

'That is our national artist, Akechi Mitsuhide,' said Kawabata, 'the one who died recently from eating *fugu* fish. How would you describe the theme of this print?'

Serdyuk's eyes slid over the figure depicted in the print, moving upwards from its exposed penis to the weights hanging on its chest.

'Yes, of course,' he said, surprising even himself. '*On* and *giri*. He's showing his prick and he's got weights round his neck.'

Kawabata clapped his hands and laughed.

'More *sake*?' he asked.

'You know,' replied Serdyuk. 'I'd be glad to, but perhaps we could do the interview first? I get drunk very quickly.'

'The interview is already over,' said Kawabata, filling the glasses. 'Let me tell you all about it. Our firm has existed for a very long time; so long, in fact, that if I told you, I'm afraid you wouldn't believe me. Our traditions are more important to us than anything. We can only be approached, if you will allow me to use a figurative expression, through a very narrow door, and you have just stepped through it with confidence. Congratulations.'

'What door's that?' asked Serdyuk.

Kawabata pointed to the print.

'That one,' he said. 'The only one which leads into Taira Incorporated.'

'I don't really understand,' said Serdyuk. 'As far as I was aware, you're traders, and for you...'

Kawabata raised an open palm. 'I am frequently horrified to observe,' he said, 'that half of Russia has already been infected with the repulsive pragmatism of the West. Present company excepted, of course, but I have good reason for saying so.'

'But what's wrong with pragmatism?' asked Serdyuk.

'In ancient times,' said Kawabata, 'in our country officials were appointed to important posts after examinations in which they wrote an essay on beauty. And this was a very wise principle, for if a man has an understanding of that which is immeasurably higher than bureaucratic procedures, then he will certainly be able to cope with lower matters. If your mind has penetrated with such lightning swiftness the mystery of the ancient allegory encoded in the drawing, then could all those price lists and overheads possibly cause you the slightest problem? Never. Moreover, after your answer I would consider it an honour to drink with you. Please do not refuse me.'

Serdyuk downed another one and found he had unexpectedly fallen into reminiscing about the previous day—it seemed he'd gone on from Pushkin Square to the Clean Ponds, but it wasn't clear to him why: all he could remember was the monument to Griboyedov, viewed from an odd perspective, as if he were looking at it from underneath a bench.

'Yes,' Kawabata was saying thoughtfully, 'if you think about it, the drawing has a terrible message. The only things that differentiate us from animals are the rules and rituals which we have agreed among ourselves. To transgress them is worse than to die, because only they separate us from the abyss of chaos which lies at our very feet—if, of course, we remove the blindfold from our eyes.'

He pointed to the print. 'But in Japan we have another tradition—sometimes, just for a second deep within ourselves, to renounce all traditions, to abandon, as we say, Buddha and Mara, in order to experience the inexpressible taste of reality. And this second sometimes produces remarkable works of art...'

Kawabata glanced once again at the man with the swords on the edge of the abyss and sighed.

'Yes,' said Serdyuk. 'Life here nowadays is enough to make a man give up on everything, too. And as for traditions...well, some people go to different kinds of churches, but of course most just watch the television and think about money.'

Serdyuk sensed that he had seriously lowered the tone of the conversation and he needed to say something clever, quickly.

'Probably,' he said, holding out his empty glass to Kawabata, 'the reason it happens is that by nature the Russian is not inclined to a search for metaphysical meaning, and makes do with a cocktail of atheism and alcoholism which, if the truth be told, is our major spiritual tradition.'

Kawabata poured again for himself and Serdyuk. 'On this point I must take the liberty of disagreeing with you,' he said. 'And this is the reason. Recently I acquired it for our collection of Russian art.'

'You collect art?' asked Serdyuk.

'Yes,' said Kawabata, rising to his feet and going over to one of the sets of shelves. 'That is also one of our firm's principles. We always attempt to penetrate the inner soul of any nation with whom we do business. It is not a matter of wishing to extract any additional profit in this way by understanding the…what's your word for it? Mentality, isn't it?'

Serdyuk nodded.

'No,' Kawabata continued, opening a large file. 'It's more a matter of a desire to raise to the level of art even those activities which are furthest removed from it. You see, if you sell a consignment of machine-guns, as it were, into empty space, then you are not very different from a cash register. But if you sell the same consignment of machine-guns to people about whom you know that every time they kill someone they have to do penance before a tripartite manifestation of the creator of the world, then the simple act of selling is exalted to the level of art. The transaction acquires a quite different quality. Not for them, of course, but for you. You are in harmony, you are at one with the universe in which you are acting, and your signature on the contract acquires the same existential status… Do I express this correctly in your language?'

Serdyuk nodded.

'The same existential status as the sunrise, the high tide or the fluttering of a blade of grass in the wind… What was I talking about to begin with?'

'About your collection.'

'Ah, that's right. Well then, would you like to take a look at this?' He held out to Serdyuk a large sheet of some material covered with a thin protective sheet of tracing paper.

'But please, be careful.'

Serdyuk took hold of the sheet. It was a piece of dusty greyish cardboard, apparently quite old. A single word had been traced on it in black paint through a crude stencil—GOD.

'What is it?'

'It's an early twentieth-century Russian conceptual icon,' said Kawabata. 'By David Burliuk. Have you heard of him?'

'I've heard the name somewhere.'

'Strangely enough, he's not very well known in Russia,' said Kawabata. 'But that's not important. Just look at it!'

Serdyuk took another look at the sheet of cardboard. The letters were dissected by white lines that must have been left by the strips of paper holding the stencil together. The word was crudely printed and there were blobs of dried paint all around it—the overall impression was strangely reminiscent of a print left by a boot.

Serdyuk looked up at Kawabata and drawled something that sounded like 'Ye-ea-es.'

'How many different meanings there are here!' Kawabata continued. 'Wait a moment, don't speak—I'll try to describe what I see, and if I miss anything, then you can add it. All right?'

Serdyuk nodded.

'Firstly,' said Kawabata, 'there is the very fact that the word "God" is printed through a stencil. That is precisely the way in which it is imprinted on a person's consciousness in childhood—as a commonplace pattern identical with the pattern imprinted on a myriad other minds. But then, a great deal depends on the quality of the surface to which it is applied—if the paper is rough and uneven, the imprint left on it will not be sharp, and if there are already other words present, it is not even clear just what mark will be left on the paper as a result. That's why they say that everyone has his own God. And then, look at the magnificent crudeness of these letters—their corners simply scratch at your eyes. It's hard to believe anyone could possibly imagine this three-letter word to be the source of the eternal love and grace, the reflection of which renders life in this world at least partially tolerable. But on the other hand, this print, which looks more like a branding mark for cattle than anything else, is the only thing a man has to set his hopes on in this life. Do you agree?'

'Yes,' said Serdyuk.

'But if that were all there was to it, this work would not be particularly outstanding—the entire range of these arguments can be encountered at any atheist lecture in a village hall. But there is one small detail which makes this icon a genuine work of genius, which sets it— and I'm not afraid to say this—above Rublyov's "Trinity". You, of course, understand what I mean, but please allow me to say it myself.'

Kawabata paused in solemn triumph. 'What I have in mind, of course, are the empty stripes left from the stencil. It would have been no trouble to colour them in—but then the result would have been so different. Yes indeed, most certainly. A person begins by looking at this word; from the appearance of sense he moves on to the visible form and suddenly he notices the blank spaces that are not filled with anything—and only there, in this nowhere, is it possible to encounter what all these huge, ugly letters strive in vain to convey, because the word "God" denominates that which cannot be denominated.

'There are many who have attempted to speak of this in words. Take Lao-tzu. But you will not find this void in Western religious painting,' Kawabata said as he poured Serdyuk another glass. 'Everything there is filled up with material objects—all kinds of curtains and folds and bowls of blood and God only knows what else. The unique vision of reality reflected in these two works of art is common only to you and us, and therefore I believe that what Russia really needs is alchemical wedlock with the East.'

'I swear to God,' said Serdyuk, 'only yesterday evening I was…'

'Precisely, with the East,' interrupted Kawabata, 'and not the West. You understand? In the depths of the Russian soul lies the same gaping void we find deep in the soul of Japan. And from this void the world comes into being, constantly, with every second. Cheers.'

Kawabata drank up, as Serdyuk had already done, and twirled the empty bottle in his fingers. 'Yes,' he said, 'most certainly, the value of a vessel lies in its emptiness. But in the last few minutes the value of this particular vessel has increased excessively. That disrupts the balance between value and the absence of value, and that is intolerable. That's what we must fear the most, a loss of balance.'

'Yes,' said Serdyuk. 'Definitely. So there's none left then?'

'We could go and get some,' Kawabata replied with a glance at his watch. 'Of course, we'd miss the football…'

'D'you follow the game?'

'I'm a Dynamo fan,' Kawabata answered, giving Serdyuk a very intimate kind of wink.

Serdyuk had long known that most of the foreigners he encountered on the streets of Moscow were not really foreigners at all, but petty trader riff-raff who'd scrabbled together a bit of cash and then tarted themselves up at the Kalinka-Stockman shop. The genuine foreigners, who had multiplied to a quite incredible extent in recent years, had been trying to dress just like the average man on the street, for reasons of personal safety. Naturally enough, most of them got their idea of what the average Moscow inhabitant on the street looked like from CNN. And in ninety cases out of a hundred, CNN, in its attempts to show Muscovites doggedly pursuing the phantom of democracy across the sun-baked desert of reform, showed close-ups of employees of the American Embassy dressed up as Muscovites, because they looked a lot more natural than Muscovites dressed up as foreigners. So although Kawabata, in an old worn jacket with a hood and rubber boots, looked exactly like a visitor from Rostov—or precisely because of this similarity—and although his face didn't look particularly Japanese, it was clear to any passer-by that he was a pure-blooded Japanese who had just slipped out of his office for a minute into the Moscow twilight.

Furthermore, Kawabata led Serdyuk along one of those routes that only foreigners use—slipping in and out of buildings, through gaps in wire fences, so that after a few minutes Serdyuk was completely disoriented. Before long they emerged on to a dark crooked street where there were several trading kiosks, and Serdyuk realized they'd reached their destination.

'What shall we get?' asked Serdyuk.

'I think a litre of *sake* would do the job,' said Kawabata. 'And a bit of grub to go with it.'

'Sake?' said Serdyuk in astonishment. 'Have they got *sake* here?'

'This is the place all right,' said Kawabata. 'There are only three kiosks in Moscow where you can get decent *sake*. Why do you think we set up our office here?'

He's joking, thought Serdyuk, and looked into the kiosk window. The selection was the usual one, except for a few unfamiliar litre bottles with labels crammed with hieroglyphics.

'Black *sake*,' Kawabata spoke gruffly. 'Two. Yes.'

Serdyuk was given one bottle, which he stuck in his pocket. Kawabata kept hold of the other one.

'Now just one other thing,' said Kawabata. 'It won't take a moment.' They walked along the line of kiosks and soon found themselves in front of a large tinplated pavilion whose door was pock-marked with holes, from bullets or nails or both. The pavilion's two windows were protected with a traditional decorative grating consisting of a metal rod bent into a semicircle at one bottom corner with rusty rays of iron radiating out from it. The sign hanging above the door said JACK OF ALL TRADES.

Inside, there were tins of enamel paint and drying-oil on the shelves, with samples of tiles hanging from the walls and a separate counter piled high with gleaming locks. But in the corner, on an upturned plastic bath, was something Serdyuk had never seen before. It was a black cuirass finished in gleaming lacquer, with small gold encrustations. Beside it lay a horned helmet with a fan of dangling neck-plates, also covered in black lacquer, and on the helmet's forehead was a gleaming five-pointed silver star. The wall beside the cuirass was hung with several swords of various lengths and a long, asymmetrical bow.

While Serdyuk was inspecting this arsenal, Kawabata engaged the salesman in quiet conversation—they seemed to be talking about arrows. Then he asked him to take down a long sword in a scabbard decorated with white diamond shapes. He drew it halfway out of the scabbard and tried the blade with his thumbnail (Serdyuk noticed that Kawabata was very careful about the way he handled the sword and even when he was testing its cutting edge, he tried not to touch the blade with his fingers). Serdyuk felt as though Kawabata had completely forgotten that he existed, so he decided to remind him.

'Tell me,' he said, turning to Kawabata, 'what could that star on the helmet mean? I suppose it's a symbol of some sort?'

'Oh yes,' said Kawabata. 'It's a symbol, and a very ancient one. It's one of the emblems of the Order of the October Star.'

Serdyuk chortled. 'What kind of order's that?' he asked. 'One they gave to the milkmaids in the ancient world?'

Kawabata gave him a long look, and the corner of his mouth turned up in an answering smile.

'No,' he said. 'This order has never been awarded by anyone to anyone. Certain people have simply realized that they are entitled to wear it. Or rather that they had always been entitled to wear it.'

'But what is it for?'

'There is nothing that it could be for.'

'The world's full of idiots, all right,' Serdyuk said vehemently.

Kawabata slammed the sword back into its scabbard. The air was suddenly thick with embarrassment.

'You're joking,' said Serdyuk, instinctively trying to smooth things over. 'You might as well have said the Order of the Red Labour Banner.'

'I have never heard of anything like that,' said Kawabata. 'The Order of the Yellow Flag certainly does exist, but that's from a quite different area. And why do you think I'm joking? I very rarely joke. And when I do, I give warning by laughing softly.'

'I'm sorry if I said something wrong,' said Serdyuk. 'It's just that I'm drunk.'

Kawabata shrugged and handed the sword back to the salesman.

'Are you taking it?' the salesman asked.

'Not this one,' said Kawabata. 'Wrap up that one over there, the small one.'

While Kawabata was paying, Serdyuk went out on to the street. He had a terrible feeling that he'd done something irredeemably stupid, but he felt calmer once he'd looked up a few times at the damp spring stars that had appeared in the sky. Then his eye was caught once again by the splayed metal rays of the window gratings and he thought sadly that when it came down to it, Russia was a land of the rising sun too—if only because the sun had never really risen over it yet. He decided this was an observation he could share with Kawabata. But by the time Kawabata emerged from the pavilion with a slim parcel tucked under his arm, this thought had already been forgotten, its place taken instead by an all-consuming desire for a drink.

Kawabata seemed to take in the situation at a glance. Moving away from the doorway, he put his bundle down beside the dark, wet trunk of a tree growing out of a hole in the asphalt and said: 'You know, of course, that in Japan we warm our *sake* before we drink it. And naturally, nobody would ever dream of drinking it straight from the bottle—that would totally contradict the spirit of the ritual. And drinking on the street is deeply dishonourable. But there is a certain ancient form which allows us to do this without losing face. It is called the "horseman's halt". It could also be translated as the "horseman's rest".'

Keeping his eyes fixed on Serdyuk's face, Kawabata drew the bottle out of his pocket.

'According to tradition,' he continued, 'the great poet Ariwara Narihira was once dispatched as hunting ambassador to the province of Ise. The road was long, and on horseback the journey took many days. It was summer. Narihira was travelling with a group of friends, and his exalted soul was filled with feelings of sadness and love. When the horsemen grew weary, they would dismount and refresh themselves with simple food and a few mouthfuls of *sake*. In order not to attract bandits, they lit no fire and drank the *sake* cold as they recited to each other marvellous verses about what they had seen on the way and what was in their hearts. And then they would set off again...'

Kawabata twisted open the screw cap.

'That is where the tradition comes from. When you drink *sake* in this fashion, you are supposed to think of the men of old, and then these thoughts should gradually merge into that radiant sadness that is born in your heart when you are aware of the fragility of this world and at the same time captivated by its beauty. So let us...'

'With pleasure,' said Serdyuk, reaching out for the bottle.

'Not so fast,' said Kawabata, jerking it away from him. 'This is the first time you have taken part in this ritual, so allow me to demonstrate the sequence of the actions involved. Do as I do and I will explain the symbolic meaning of what is happening.'

Kawabata set down the bottle beside his bundle.

'First of all we must tether our horses,' he said.

He tugged at the tree's lowest branch to test its strength and then wove his hands around it as though he was winding a string on to it. Serdyuk realized he was supposed to do the same. Reaching up to a branch a little higher, he roughly repeated Kawabata's manipulations under his watchful gaze.

'No,' said Kawabata, 'he's uncomfortable like that.'

'Who?' asked Serdyuk.

'Your horse. You've tethered him too high. How will he graze? Remember, it's not just you that's resting, it's your faithful companion as well.'

Serdyuk looked puzzled, and Kawabata sighed. 'You must understand,' he said patiently, 'that in performing this ritual we are transported back, as it were, to the Heian era. At present we are riding through the summer countryside to the province of Ise. I ask you, please, retie the bridle.'

Serdyuk decided it would be best not to argue. He waved his hands over the upper branch and then wove them around the lower one.

'That's much better,' said Kawabata. 'And now we should compose verses about what we see around us.'

He closed his eyes and waited in silence for several seconds, then pronounced a long, guttural phrase in which Serdyuk was unable to detect either rhythm or rhyme.

'That's more or less about what we've been saying,' he explained. 'About invisible horses nibbling at invisible grass and about how it's far more real than this asphalt which, in essence, does not exist. But in general it's all built on wordplay. Now it's your turn.'

Serdyuk suddenly felt miserable. 'I really don't know what to say,' he said in an apologetic tone. 'I don't write poems, I don't even like them much. And who needs words with stars up in the sky?'

'Oh,' Kawabata exclaimed, 'magnificent! Magnificent! How right you are! Only thirty-two syllables, but worth an entire book!'

He took a step backwards and bowed twice.

'And how good that I recited my verse first!' he said. 'After you I wouldn't have dared to do it! But where did you learn to write *tanka*?'

'Oh, around,' Serdyuk said evasively.

Kawabata held out the bottle to him. Serdyuk took several large gulps and handed it back. Kawabata also applied himself eagerly, drinking in small sips, holding his free hand behind him—there was obviously some ritual meaning to the gesture, but to be on the safe side Serdyuk avoided asking any questions. While Kawabata was drinking, he lit a cigarette. Two or three drags restored his self-confidence and he even began to feel slightly ashamed of his recent timidity.

'And by the way, about the horse,' he said. 'I didn't actually tether him too high. It's just that recently I've been getting tired very quickly, and I take halts of up to three days at a time. That's why he has a long bridle. Otherwise he'd eat all the grass on the first day.'

Kawabata's face changed. He bowed once more, walked off to one side and began unfastening the buttons of his jacket over his stomach.

'What are you doing?' asked Serdyuk.

'I am so ashamed,' said Kawabata. 'I can't carry on living after suffering such dishonour.'

He sat down on the asphalt, unwrapped the bundle, took out the sword and bared its blade—a glimmering patch of lilac slithered along it, reflected from the neon lamp above their heads. Serdyuk finally realized what Kawabata was about to do and managed to grab hold of his hands.

'Stop that, please,' he said in genuine fright. 'How can you give such importance to trifles?'

'Will you be able to forgive me?' Kawabata asked emotionally, rising to his feet.

'Please, let's just forget about this stupid misunderstanding. And anyway, a love of animals is a noble feeling. Why should you be ashamed of that?'

Kawabata thought for a moment and the wrinkles on his brow disappeared.

'You're right,' he said. 'I really was motivated by sympathy for a tired animal, not the desire to show that I understood something better than you. There really is nothing dishonourable about that. I may have said something stupid, but I have not lost face.'

He put the sword back into its scabbard, swayed on his feet and applied himself to the bottle once again.

'If some petty misunderstanding should arise between two noble men, surely it will crumble to dust if they both attack it with the keen edge of their minds,' he said, handing the bottle to Serdyuk.

Serdyuk finished off what was left.

'Of course it will,' he said. 'That's as clear as day, that is.'

Kawabata raised his head and looked dreamily up at the sky.

'And who needs words with stars up in the sky?' he declaimed. 'How very fine. You know, I would really like to celebrate this remarkable moment with a gesture of some kind. Why don't we release our horses? Let them graze on this beautiful plain and retreat into the mountains during the nights. Surely they have deserved their freedom?'

'You're a very kind-hearted man,' said Serdyuk.

Kawabata walked unsteadily over to the tree, drew the sword from its scabbard and sliced off the lower branch with a movement that was almost invisible. It fell on to the pavement. Kawabata waved his arms in the air and shouted something loud and incomprehensible—Serdyuk realized he was driving away the horses. Then he came back, picked up the bottle and with disappointment tipped out the last few drops on to the ground.

'It's getting cold,' Serdyuk observed, looking around and instinctively sensing that any moment now the damp Moscow air would weave itself into the solid shape of a police patrol. 'Shouldn't we be getting back to the office?'

'Of course,' said Kawabata, 'of course. And we can have a bite to eat there too.'

Serdyuk didn't remember the way back at all. He only became aware of himself again when they were sitting on the floor of the room from which their journey had started. They were eating noodles out of soup plates. The second bottle was already half empty, but Serdyuk realized he was completely sober and in a distinctly exalted mood. Kawabata must have been feeling good as well, because he was humming quietly and beating time with his chopsticks, sending slim vermicelli snakes flying off in all directions. Some of them landed on Serdyuk, but he didn't find it annoying.

When he'd finished, Kawabata set his plate aside and turned towards Serdyuk.

'Now tell me,' he said, 'what does a man want after returning home from a dangerous journey, once he has satisfied his hunger and thirst?'

'I don't know,' said Serdyuk. 'Round here they usually turn on the television.'

'Nah-ah,' said Kawabata. 'In Japan we make the finest televisions in the world, but that doesn't prevent us from realizing that a television is just a small transparent window in the pipe of a spiritual garbage chute. I wasn't thinking of those unfortunates who spend their whole lives in a trance watching an endless stream of swill and only feeling alive when they recognize a familiar tin can. I'm talking about people who are worthy of mention in our conversation.'

Kawabata screwed up his eyes, moved closer to Serdyuk and smiled. 'You remember, just a little while ago, when we set the horses loose, then forded the Tenzin River and walked on foot to the gates of Rasemon, you were talking of the warmth of another body lying beside you? Surely this is what your spirit was seeking at that moment?'

Serdyuk shuddered. He's gay, he thought, I should have guessed it right from the start.

Kawabata moved even closer. 'After all, it is one of the few remaining natural feelings which a man may still experience. And we did agree that what Russia needs is alchemical wedlock with the East, didn't we?'

'We did,' said Serdyuk, squirming inwardly. 'Of course it does. I was just thinking about it only yesterday.'

'Good,' said Kawabata, 'but there is nothing that happens to nations and countries that is not repeated in symbolic form in the life of the individuals who live in those countries and make up those nations. Russia, in the final analysis, is you. So if you spoke sincerely, and of course I cannot believe otherwise, then let us perform this ritual immediately. Let us, as it were, reinforce our words and thoughts with a symbolic fusion of basic principles...'

Kawabata bowed and winked.

'In any case, we shall be working together, and there is nothing which brings men so close together as...'

He winked again and smiled. Serdyuk bared his teeth mechanically in response and noticed that one of Kawabata's own teeth was missing. But there were other things that struck him as far more significant: first of all, Serdyuk remembered the danger of Aids, and then he recalled that his underwear wasn't particularly clean. Kawabata got up and went across to the cupboard, rummaged in it and tossed Serdyuk a piece of cloth. It was a blue cap, exactly like those shown on the heads of the men on the *sake* glasses. Kawabata put one on his head, gestured for Serdyuk to do the same and clapped his hands.

Immediately one of the wall panels slid to one side and Serdyuk became aware of rather wild-sounding music. Behind the panel, in a room the size of a broom cupboard, was a group of four or five girls wearing long colourful kimonos and holding musical instruments. The girls waved their heads from side to side and smiled as they played. One had a balalaika, another was banging together a pair of painted wooden Palekh spoons, and two more were holding small plastic harmonicas which made a fearful, piercing, squeaking noise. This was only natural, Serdyuk thought, since harmonicas like that were never actually made to play on, merely to create a happy atmosphere at children's parties.

The girls' smiles were a little forced and the layer of rouge on their cheeks a bit too thick. Their features were not even slightly Japanese—they were just ordinary Russian girls, and not even particularly beautiful, either. One of them looked like a student from Serdyuk's year at college, a girl called Masha.

'Woman,' Kawabata said thoughtfully, 'is by no means created for our downfall. In that marvellous moment when she envelops us in her body, it is as though we are transported to that happy land from which we came and to which we shall return after death. I love women and I am not ashamed to admit it. And every time I am joined with one of them, it is as though I...'

Without bothering to finish, he clapped his hands and the girls danced forward in close formation, gazing straight ahead into empty space as they moved directly towards Serdyuk.

'Sixth rank, fifth rank, fourth rank, and now our horses turn to the left, and the longed-for palace of Suzdaku emerges from the mist,' said Kawabata as he buttoned up his pants, gazing attentively all the while at Serdyuk.

Serdyuk raised his head from the floor covering. He must have fallen asleep for a few minutes—Kawabata was obviously continuing with some story, but Serdyuk couldn't remember the beginning. He took a look at himself. He was wearing nothing but an old washed-out T-shirt with Olympic symbols on it; the rest of his clothing was scattered about the room. The girls, tousled, half naked and passionless, were fussing around an electric kettle that was boiling in the corner. Serdyuk started getting dressed quickly.

'Further on, by the left wing of the castle,' Kawabata continued, 'we take a turn to the right, and there are the gates of Blissful Light rushing towards us... And now everything depends on which poetic style is in the closest harmony with your soul at this moment. If you are inwardly attuned to simplicity and joy, you will gallop straight forward. If your thoughts are far removed from this frail and perishable world, then you will turn to the left and see before you the gates of Eternal Peace. And finally, if you are young and hot-headed and your soul thirsts for delights, you will turn to the right and enter in at the gates of Enduring Joy.'

Squirming under Kawabata's unwavering gaze, Serdyuk pulled on his trousers, his shirt and his jacket, and began knotting the tie round his neck, but his fingers got tangled up in the knots and he gave up, dragged the tie off over his head and shoved it back into his pocket.

'But then,' Kawabata continued, raising one finger in a solemn gesture—he seemed so absorbed in what he was saying that Serdyuk realized there was no need to feel embarrassed or hurry—'then, whatever gateway you may have chosen to enter the Imperial palace, you find yourself in the same courtyard! Think of what a revelation this is for a man accustomed to reading the language of symbols! Whatever road your heart has followed, whatever route your soul may have mapped out, you always return to the same thing! Remember what is said—all things return to the one, but where does the one return to? Ah?'

Serdyuk raised his eyes from the floor.

'Well, where does the one return to?' Kawabata repeated, and his eyes narrowed into two slits.

Serdyuk coughed and opened his mouth to say something, but before he could speak Kawabata had clapped his hands in delight.

'Oh,' he said, 'profound and accurate as always.'

Kawabata took a step backwards and added yet another bow to the long sequence he had already made that evening. There seemed to be tears gleaming in his eyes.

'Oh, how ashamed I am that I have subjected you to the insult of this interrogation!' he said.

He glanced across at the girls sitting round the electric kettle and clapped his hands twice. The girls gathered up the kettle and their scattered clothes and quickly disappeared into the broom cupboard.

'Such are the rules of our firm,' Kawabata finished his sentence. 'I've already told you that when I use the word "firm" I am not translating absolutely accurately. In actual fact it would be more correct to say "clan". But if this term is used too early, it may arouse suspicion and fear. We therefore prefer first to find out what kind of man we are dealing with and then go into the details. Even though in your case the answer was clear to me from the moment when you recited that magical poem...'

Kawabata stood absolutely still and closed his eyes, and for several seconds his lips moved silently. Serdyuk guessed that he was repeating the phrase about the stars in the sky, which Serdyuk couldn't remember exactly himself.

'Quite remarkable words. Yes, from that moment on everything was absolutely clear to me. But there are rules, very strict rules, and I was obliged to ask you the required questions. Now I must tell you the following,' Kawabata continued. 'To put it simply, we accept you as a member of our clan, which is one of the most ancient in Japan. The title of the vacant post which you will occupy is "Assistant Manager for the Northern Barbarians". I understand that the title might possibly seem offensive to you, but this is a tradition older than the city of Moscow. This is a post for a *samurai*, and a layman may not occupy it. Therefore, if you are willing to accept the post, I will make you a *samurai*.'

'But what kind of work is it?'

'Oh, nothing complicated,' said Kawabata. 'Papers, clients. From the outside it all looks just the same as in any other firm, except that your inner attitude to events must match the harmony of the cosmos.'

'And what's the pay like?'

'You will receive two hundred and fifty *koku* of rice a year,' said Kawabata, and frowned as he calculated something in his head. 'That's about forty thousand of your dollars.'

'In dollars?'

'However you wish,' Kawabata said with a shrug.

'I'll take it,' said Serdyuk.

'As I expected. Now tell me, are you ready to accept that you are a *samurai* of the Taira clan?'

'I should say so.'

'Are you willing to link your life and your death with the destiny of our clan?'

All these crazy rituals they have, thought Serdyuk. Where do they find the time to make all those televisions?

'I am,' he said.

'Will you be prepared, as a real man, to cast the ephemeral blossom of this life over the edge of the abyss and into the void if this is required of you by your *giri*?' Kawabata asked with a nod in the direction of the print on the wall.

Serdyuk took another look at it.

'I will,' he said, 'of course. Chuck the blossom down the abyss—no problem.'

'You swear?'

'I swear.'

'Splendid,' said Kawabata, 'splendid. Now there is only one small formality left and we'll be finished. We must receive confirmation from Japan. But that will only take a few minutes.'

He sat down facing the fax machine, rummaged through a pile of papers until he found a clean sheet, and then a brush appeared in his hand.

Serdyuk changed position. His legs had gone numb from sitting too long on the floor and he thought it would be a good idea to ask Kawabata whether he would be allowed to bring a stool—just a small one—to work with him. Then he looked around for the remains of the *sake*, but the bottle had disappeared. Kawabata was busy with his sheet of paper and Serdyuk was afraid to ask—he couldn't be sure that he wouldn't disrupt the ritual.

He remembered the oath he had just taken. God almighty, he thought, the number of oaths I've sworn in my life! Promised to struggle for the cause of the Communist Party, didn't I? Half a dozen times, probably, going back to when I was just a kid. Promised to marry Masha, didn't I? Sure I did. And yesterday, after the Clean Ponds, when I was drinking with those idiots, didn't I promise we'd get another bottle on me? And now look where it's got me—chucking blossoms down an abyss.

Meanwhile, Kawabata finished pushing his brush around the sheet of paper, blew on it and showed it to Serdyuk. It was a large chrysanthemum drawn in black ink.

'What is it?' asked Serdyuk.

'Oh,' said Kawabata, 'it's a chrysanthemum. You understand, when a new member joins us, it is such a great joy for the entire Taira clan that it would be inappropriate to entrust it to marks on paper. In such cases, we usually inform our leaders by drawing a flower. What's more, this is the very flower of which we were just speaking. It symbolizes your life, which now belongs to the Taira clan, and at the same time it testifies to your final awareness of its fleeting ephemerality…'

'I get it,' said Serdyuk.

Kawabata blew on the sheet of paper once more, then set it in the crack of the fax machine and began dialling an extremely long number. He got through only at the third attempt. The fax hummed into life, a little green lamp on its corner lit up and the page slowly disappeared.

Kawabata stared fixedly at the machine without moving or changing his pose. Several long and weary minutes went by, and then the fax began to hum again and another sheet of paper slid out from underneath its black body. Serdyuk understood immediately that this was the reply.

Kawabata waited until the full length of the page had emerged and then tore it out of the fax, glanced at it and looked slowly round at Serdyuk.

'Congratulations,' he said, 'my sincere congratulations! The reply is most propitious.'

He held out the sheet of paper to Serdyuk, who took it and saw a different drawing—this time it was a long, slightly bent stick with some kind of pattern on it and something protruding from one side.

'What is it?' he asked.

'It's a sword,' Kawabata said solemnly, 'the symbol of your new status in life. And since I never had any doubt that this would be the outcome, allow me to present you, so to speak, with your passport.'

With these words Kawabata held out the short sword he had bought earlier in the tinplated pavilion.

Perhaps it was Kawabata's fixed, unblinking stare, or perhaps it was the result of some chemical reaction in his own alcohol-drenched metabolism, but for some reason Serdyuk became suddenly aware of the significance and solemnity of the moment. He almost went down on his knees, but just in time he remembered that it was the medieval European knights who did that, not the Japanese—and not even the knights, if he thought about it, but only the actors from the Odessa film studios who were playing them in some intolerably dreary old Soviet film. So he just held out his hands and took a cautious grip on the cold instrument of death. There was a design on the scabbard that he hadn't noticed before: it was a drawing of three cranes in flight—the gold wire impressed into the black lacquer of the scabbard traced a light and dashing contour of exceptional beauty.

'Your soul,' said Kawabata, gazing into Serdyuk's eyes again, 'lies in this scabbard.'

'What a beautiful drawing,' said Serdyuk. 'It reminds me of a song I know, about cranes. How does it go, now? "And in their flight I see a narrow space, perhaps that is a place for me..."'

'Yes, yes,' Kawabata cut in. 'And why would a man need any more? The Lord Buddha can easily fit the entire world with all its problems into the space between two cranes. Why, it would be lost in the spaces between the feathers of either of them... How poetical this evening is! Why don't we have another drink? For the space in the flight of cranes which you have finally occupied?'

Serdyuk thought he sensed something ominous in Kawabata's words, but he paid no attention, because Kawabata could hardly have known the song was about the souls of dead soldiers.

'Gladly,' said Serdyuk, 'in just a while. I...'

Suddenly there was a loud knock at the door. Kawabata turned and shouted something in Japanese, the panel slid to one side and a man's face, also with southern features, appeared in the gap. The face said something and Kawabata nodded.

'I shall have to leave you for a few minutes,' he said to Serdyuk. 'It seems there is some serious news coming in. If you wish, please look through any of the print albums while you are waiting,'—he nodded in the direction of the bookshelf—'or simply amuse yourself.'

Serdyuk nodded. Kawabata quickly left the room and closed the panel behind him. It was quiet in the building. Behind the sliding panel Serdyuk could hear the whispers of the girls swearing at each other; they were very close, but he could hardly make out any of their obscenities, and the muffled voices mingled together to produce a gentle, calming, rustling sound, as though there was a garden behind the wall and the leaves of the blossoming cherries were murmuring in the wind.

Serdyuk was woken by a low moaning. He couldn't tell how long he'd been asleep, but it must have been quite a long time— Kawabata was sitting in the centre of the room, already changed and shaved. He was wearing a white shirt and his hair, so recently tousled and untidy, was combed back neatly. He was the source of the moaning that had woken Serdyuk. It was some kind of mournful dirge. Kawabata was holding the long sword in his hands and wiping it with a white piece of cloth. Serdyuk noticed that Kawabata's shirt was unbuttoned and his hairless chest and belly were exposed.

Kawabata realized that Serdyuk had woken up and turned to face him with a broad smile.

'Did you sleep well?' he asked.

'I wasn't exactly sleeping,' said Serdyuk, 'I just…'

'Had a doze,' said Kawabata, 'I understand. All of us are merely dozing in this life. And we only wake when it ends. Do you recall how we forded the brook when we were walking back to the office?'

'Yes,' said Serdyuk, 'that stream coming out of the pipe.'

'Pipe or no pipe, that is not important. Do you recall the bubbles on the surface of that brook?'

'Yes. They were big ones all right.'

'Truly,' said Kawabata, raising the blade to the level of his eyes and gazing at it intently, 'truly this world is like bubbles on the water. Is that not so?'

Serdyuk thought that Kawabata was right, and he wanted very much to say something so that his companion would realize how well he understood his feelings and how completely he shared them.

'Not even that,' he said, raising himself up on one elbow. 'It's like…let me think now… It's like a photograph of those bubbles that has fallen down behind a chest of drawers and been gnawed by the rats.'

Kawabata smiled once again.

'You are a genuine poet,' he said. 'I have no doubt at all about that.'

'And what's more,' Serdyuk went on, inspired, 'it could well be that the rats got to it even before it had been developed.'

'Splendid,' said Kawabata, 'quite splendid. This is the poetry of words, but there is also the poetry of deeds. I hope that your final poem without words will prove a match for the verses which have brought me so much delight today.'

'What d'you mean?'

Kawabata carefully set his sword down on a bamboo mat.

'Life is uncertain and changeable,' he said thoughtfully. 'In the early morning no one can say what awaits him in the evening.'

'Has something happened, then?'

'Oh, yes. You know, of course, that business is like war. The Taira clan has an enemy, a mighty enemy—Minamoto.'

'Minamoto?' echoed Serdyuk, feeling a shiver run down his spine. 'And?'

'Today news came that cunning treachery on the Tokyo stock exchange has allowed the Minamoto Group to acquire a controlling interest in Taira Incorporated. A certain English bank and the Singapore mafia were involved, but that is not important. We are destroyed. And our enemy is triumphant.'

Serdyuk said nothing for a while as he tried to work out what this meant. Only one thing was clear, though—it didn't mean anything good.

'But you and I,' said Kawabata, 'we two *samurai* of the clan of Taira—surely we shall not allow our spirits to be overcast by the shifting shadows of these insignificant bubbles of existence?'

'Er...no,' Serdyuk answered.

Kawabata laughed fiercely and his eyes flashed.

'No,' he said. 'Minamoto shall not behold our degradation and dishonour. One should leave this life as the white cranes disappear into the clouds. Let not a single petty feeling remain in our hearts at a moment of such beauty.'

He swung round sharply where he sat, turning the bamboo mat with him, and bowed to Serdyuk.

'I wish to ask you a favour,' he said. 'When I rip open my belly, please cut off my head!'

'What?'

'My head, please cut off my head. We call this rendering the final service. And a *samurai* who is asked to do this may not refuse without covering himself in great dishonour.'

'But I never… That is, before…'

'It's very simple. One stroke and it's done. Wh-oo-oosh!'

Kawabata waved his hands rapidly through the air.

'But I am afraid I won't manage it,' said Serdyuk. 'I don't have any experience of that kind of thing.'

Kawabata pondered for a moment, then suddenly his face darkened as though he had been struck by some exceptionally unpleasant thought. He slapped his hand against his *tatami*.

'It's good that I am leaving this life soon,' he said, looking up guiltily at Serdyuk. 'What a coarse and ignorant brute I am!'

He covered his face with his hands and began rocking from side to side.

Serdyuk quietly stood up, tiptoed over to the screen, silently slid it to one side and went out into the corridor. The cold concrete felt unpleasant under his bare feet, and Serdyuk suddenly realized that while he and Kawabata had been wandering around dark and dubious alleyways in search of *sake*, his socks and shoes had been standing in the corridor by the door, where he'd left them in the afternoon; he couldn't remember what he'd been wearing on his feet at all, just as he couldn't recall how he and Kawabata had got out on to the street or how they'd got back in.

'Out, I've got to get out right now,' he thought as he turned the corner in the corridor. 'First I get out, then there'll be time for a bit of thinking.'

The security guard rose from his stool as Serdyuk approached.

'And where are we off to at a time like this?' he asked with a yawn. 'It's half past three in the morning.'

'We got a bit involved,' said Serdyuk. 'You know, with the interview.'

'OK then,' said the security guard. 'Let's have your pass.'

'What pass?'

'To get out.'

'But you let me in without any pass.'

'That's right,' said the security guard, 'but to get out, you need a pass.'

The lamp on the desk cast a dim glow on Serdyuk's shoes standing over by the wall. The door was only a yard away from them, and beyond the door lay freedom. Serdyuk took a small step towards the shoes. Then another one. The security guard cast an indifferent glance at his bare feet.

'And then,' he said, toying with his rubber truncheon, 'we've got regulations. The alarm's on. The door's locked until eight o'clock in the morning. If I open it the cops'll be round in a flash. That means hassle, official statements. So I can't open up. Not unless there's a fire. Or a flood.'

'But this world,' Serdyuk began ingratiatingly, 'is like bubbles on the water.'

The security guard laughed and shook his head.

'Sure, sure,' he said. 'We know what kind of place it is we work in. But you've got to understand where I'm coming from. Just imagine that along with those bubbles there's a set of instructions drifting along on the water. And just as long as it's reflected in one of those bubbles, we lock up at eleven and open the door at eight. And that's it.'

'So what am I supposed to do?' Serdyuk asked.

'What can you do? Wait until eight. And ask them to write you out a pass.'

Serdyuk cast a final glance at the security guard's burly shoulders and the truncheon in his hands, then slowly turned on his heel and started trudging back to Kawabata's room.

'Listen,' the security guard called out behind him, 'better not go walking about without your *geta*. The floor in here's concrete. You'll get a chill in your kidneys.'

When he reached Kawabata's office again and silently slid the panel open, Serdyuk noticed there was a strong smell in the room of stale drink and female sweat. Kawabata was still sitting there on the floor, his face in his hands, rocking from side to side, as though he hadn't even noticed that Serdyuk had gone out.

'Mr Kawabata,' Serdyuk called quietly. Kawabata lowered his hands.

'Are you feeling bad?'

'I feel terrible,' said Kawabata, 'I feel absolutely terrible. If I had a hundred bellies, I would slit them all without a moment's delay. Never in my life have I felt such shame as I am feeling now.'

'Why, what's the problem?' Serdyuk asked sympathetically, kneeling down to face the Japanese.

'I made bold to ask you to render me the final service without thinking that there would be no one to render the service to you if I commit *seppuku* first. Such monstrous dishonour.'

'Me?' said Serdyuk, rising to his feet, 'me?'

'Why yes,' said Kawabata, also rising and fixing Serdyuk with his blazing eyes. 'Who will cut off your head? Not Grisha, I suppose?'

'Who's Grisha?'

'The security guard. You were just talking to him. He's no good for anything except breaking heads with his truncheon. The rules say it has to be cut off, and not just any old way, it has to be left hanging on a scrap of skin. Imagine how terrible it would look if it went rolling across the floor! But sit down, sit down.'

There was such hypnotic power in Kawabata's gaze that Serdyuk involuntarily lowered himself on to a bamboo mat. It was all he could do to tear his eyes away from Kawabata's face.

'And anyway, I suspect you don't know what the doctrine of the direct and fearless return to eternity tells us about *seppuku*,' said Kawabata.

'What?'

'Do you know how to slit open your belly?'

'No,' said Serdyuk, staring blankly at the wall.

'There are various ways of doing it. The simplest is a horizontal incision. But there's nothing special in that. A vertical incision is a little bit better, but that's the lower-middle-class style, and it's a bit provincial too. You can use crossed incisions, but I wouldn't advise that either. Two years ago a double parallel incision was all the fashion, but that's difficult. So what I would suggest is a long diagonal cut from the lower left to the upper right with a slight turn back towards the centre at the end. From the strictly aesthetic point of view it's quite beyond reproach, and when you've done it, I'll probably do it the same way.'

Serdyuk attempted to stand up, but Kawabata placed a hand on his shoulder and forced him back down.

'Unfortunately, we shall have to do everything in a hurry,' he said with a sigh. 'We don't have any white blinds or anything suitable to smoke. There are no warriors with drawn swords waiting at the edge of the platform… We do have Grisha, I suppose, but then, what kind of a warrior is he? Anyway, they're not really necessary, they're there only in case a *samurai* betrays his oath and refuses to commit *seppuku*. Then they beat him to death like a dog. There haven't been any cases like that in my time—but then, it's really beautiful when there are men with drawn swords standing around the border of the fenced-off area, the sun glinting on their steel. Yes, perhaps… Do you want me to call Grisha? And maybe Semyon from the first floor as well? To bring it closer to the original ritual?'

'Don't bother,' said Serdyuk.

'That's right,' said Kawabata, 'that's right. Of course, you understand that the most important thing in any ritual is not the external form, but the internal content that fills it.'

'I understand, I understand. I understand everything,' said Serdyuk, staring with hatred at Kawabata.

'I am therefore absolutely certain that everything will proceed excellently.'

Kawabata lifted the short sword he had bought from the floor, drew it out of its scabbard and sliced through the air a couple of times.

'It will do,' he said. 'Now let me tell you something. There are always two problems. Not to fall over on your back after the incision—that's really most inelegant, but I can help you there—and the other problem is not to catch the spinal column with the blade. Therefore the blade should not be inserted too far. Let's do it this way…'

He picked up several sheets of paper with fax messages on them—Serdyuk noticed that the sheet with the drawing of the chrysanthemum was among them—stacked them into a neat pile and then carefully wrapped them round the blade, leaving four or five inches of steel projecting.

'That's it. So, you take the handle in your right hand, and you hold it here with your left hand. You don't need to push it in very hard, or it might get stuck and then… All right, and then upwards to the right. And now you probably want to focus your mind. We don't have much time, but at least there's enough for that.'

Serdyuk was sitting there in a kind of a trance, staring at the wall. Feeble thoughts ran through his head about pushing Kawabata aside and running out into the corridor and… But the door out there was locked, and there was Grisha with his truncheon. And there was supposed to be someone called Semyon on the first floor, too. In theory he could phone the police, but Kawabata was right there beside him with his sword… And the police wouldn't turn out at this hour of the night. But the most unpleasant thing of all was that any such course of action would bring an expression of astonishment to Kawabata's face, followed rapidly by a grimace of fierce contempt. There was something in what had happened that day which Serdyuk didn't want to betray, and he even knew what it was—it was that moment after they'd tethered their horses, when they recited poetry to each other. And even though, if he really thought about it, there hadn't actually been any horses or any poems, the moment had been real, and so had the wind from the south that brought the promise of summer, and the stars in the sky. There couldn't be the slightest doubt that it had all been real—that is, just the way it should have been. But as for the world waiting for him behind that door which was due to be opened at eight in the morning…

Serdyuk's thoughts paused briefly, and he could suddenly hear quiet noises all around him. Kawabata's stomach was gurgling as he sat there beside the fax with his eyes closed, and Serdyuk thought that his companion was sure to complete the entire procedure with brilliant ease. And the world that the Japanese was preparing to quit—if by 'world' we mean everything that a man can feel and experience in his life—was certainly far more attractive than the stinking streets of Moscow that closed in on Serdyuk every morning to the accompaniment of the songs of Filipp Kirkorov.

Serdyuk realized why he'd suddenly thought of Kirkorov—the

girls sitting behind the wall were listening to one of his songs. Then he heard the sounds of a brief quarrel, stifled weeping and the click of a switch. The invisible television began transmitting a news programme, but it seemed to Serdyuk that the channel hadn't really changed and Kirkorov had simply stopped singing and begun talking in a quiet voice. Then he heard one of the girls whispering agitatedly:

'He is, look! Pissed again! Look at him embracing Chirac! I tell you, he's pissed as a newt!'

Serdyuk thought for a few more seconds.

'Ah, to hell with the lot of it,' he said decisively. 'Give me the sword.'

Kawabata walked quickly over to him, went down on one knee and held out the handle of the sword to him.

'Hang on,' said Serdyuk, and he unbuttoned his shirt under his jacket. 'Can I do it through the T-shirt?'

Kawabata thought for a moment.

'It has been done on occasion. In 1454 after he lost the battle of Okehajama, Takeda Katsueri slit open his belly through his hunting costume. So it's OK.'

Serdyuk took hold of the sword. □

 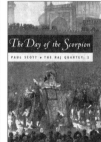 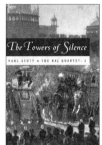 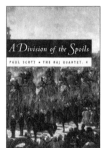

GRANTA

BURYING THE BONES
Orlando Figes

Sarcophagi containing the remains of Russia's last Tsar and his family ASSOCIATED PRESS

'How long did he rule for anyway?' The question from a man in a Yankees baseball cap was met by silence from his fellow Russians. Did anybody know? We were a small crowd waiting in the late afternoon sun for the cortège of black cars carrying the bones of the last Tsar and his descendants to arrive at the Troitsky Gates of the Peter and Paul Fortress. The Romanovs were late and most of the people around me were coming home from work when they came across the police barriers on Troitsky Square which should have cleared by three. There was a long silence. None of these commuters, it seemed, knew their history. Then an old man (who looked like a professor) spoke out in a voice of authority: 'Nicholas ruled for thirty-five years.' Someone immediately disagreed: 'It was less than that.' But nobody was sure.

The people of St Petersburg were not much disturbed by the burial of the bones of Nicholas II—who ruled Russia from 1894 to 1917—aside from the traffic jams it caused. The next day, 17 July, the day of the funeral itself, the Nevsky Prospekt was gridlocked when I set off for the ceremony. I had come to the city for a week to report on the funeral for a German newspaper, and to finish a book I had been writing with a Russian friend on the political culture of 1917. I stepped out into the middle of the traffic, opened the door of the nearest car, and took the driver's nod towards the empty seat as an invitation to get in. Every car in Russia is a part-time taxi. I've had rides in lorries and snow-clearers, the ZIL limousines of the old Party chiefs, and ambulances—although not (as yet) one with patients inside.

My driver—a suntanned watermelon trader in shorts and a string vest—was not in a good mood. He was cursing Boris Yeltsin, whose motorcade was at this moment speeding through the police-cordoned streets, as his own clapped-out Lada repeatedly stalled. 'Get a move on,' he shouted through the window to the bus in front of us. 'These can't wait all day.' He was referring to the melons piled up on the back seat. I asked him what he thought of the funeral. 'What am I to think? I don't have time to think. The Tsar will be able to go to heaven. I am glad for him. Life up there is better than down here.'

In 1998, most Russians had too many contemporary problems to be bothered by the events of eighty years before. Political turbulence, poverty, crime, unpaid wages—who, in these circumstances, would worry about the fate of the Romanovs? Yet the funeral held a kind of passive interest for the people of St Petersburg (one poll suggested that nearly half the city's residents intended to watch it on television) and there was a general sense that the burial was right.

But would I make it to the ceremony? It seemed not; the traffic was still not moving and my driver still cursing. I paid him off and settled in a bar on the Nevsky Prospekt where a small group were watching the live broadcast on a portable television. 'I think it's right that they should have a Christian burial,' said the peroxide blonde behind the bar as she poured me out a beer. 'It is a matter of human decency.' She was wearing a necklace with a cross together with a silver chain made up of the letters G-U-C-C-I. 'It's the children I feel sorry for,' said a businessman as we watched another sequence of sepia photographs of the Tsar and his daughters playing tennis and rowing in a boat. 'The Communists were savages to murder them.'

Then we heard the Russian President give his funeral oration. This was Yeltsin at his most solemn and articulate. The murder of the Tsar was 'a shameful act which the Communists concealed'. His family were 'innocent victims of repression' which should have no more place in Russian history. Their burial was a 'symbolic moment of national repentance and unity'. It was 'time to tell the truth…we are all guilty'. We watched as Yeltsin slowly bowed down before the congregation of Romanovs and only then did it become clear that those words, for him, were more than a cliché. In his old life, as the Party boss of Sverdlovsk (Yekaterinburg), Yeltsin himself had ordered the destruction of the Ipatiev House, where Nicholas and his family were murdered by the Bolsheviks in the small hours of the morning of 17 July 1918. This was a personal repentance. I looked across at the blonde behind the bar and her eyes were full of tears.

The Tsar and his family were the first victims of the Terror which their deaths announced. The slaughter of the children, in particular, has become a symbol of the moral degradation of a regime which went on to kill millions of other innocent people who do not have a grave that anybody knows. This is a nation, like the Jews, where nearly every family has part of itself missing—grandparents who died 'in the camps' or disappeared in the war—and no place to mourn and commemorate that loss. I bought a cognac for Nastya, the tearful barmaid, and she began to tell me about her grandfather. He was arrested in 1938.

Unfinished business—that is what the bones are all about. For seventy years the nine skeletons (of the Tsar, his wife, and three of his daughters, along with a cook, a maid, a valet and the family physician) had rotted underground in a wooded spot twelve miles north-west of Yekaterinburg. The records suggest that the corpses of Alexis, the Tsar's only son, and a fourth daughter, Maria, were burned to ashes by their executioners, but that in the rush to dispose of all the bodies before the White forces arrived in the city they had simply buried the other skeletons. The Bolsheviks said nothing about the murder—other than a mendacious official announcement that the former Tsar had been executed and his wife and son removed to a 'safe place'. This, after all, had long been planned as a secret execution. Lenin, who it seems had ordered it, rejected the idea of a trial or public execution—such as the Jacobins had given Louis XVI in 1793 or the English revolutionaries Charles I in 1649—on the grounds that a trial would presuppose the possibility of his innocence (and that in effect would put the Bolsheviks on trial). For seven decades his successors hid the truth—until the bones were finally exhumed in 1991 (twelve years after their discovery by a geologist named Alexander Avdonin) and subjected for the next six years to forensic tests around the world. By comparing their DNA to that of the Tsar and Tsarina's relatives, including the Duke of Edinburgh (Empress Alexandra's great-nephew), scientists are as sure as scientists can be that these are the bones of the Romanovs.

Truth and national reconciliation. One can only hope that this act of burial will close an awful century of Russian history. But one also suspects, as many Russians have told me, that the conflicts of the past will not be overcome until Lenin is buried in the ground as well. His wax-like body remains in the mausoleum on Red Square. Yet the frequent calls by many different groups for him to be removed and laid to rest alongside his mother's grave in St Petersburg (as Lenin had himself apparently requested) have been bitterly opposed with bombs and violent threats by the Communists. In Russia, it appears, there are still too many people who will not forget the past.

The Communists are still the country's largest and best-organized party, with at least one-quarter of the votes and slightly more seats in the parliament. 'Bloody Nicholas' is the crucial figure of their mythology—founded as that is on the 'Bloody Sunday' massacre of 1905, the Lena massacre of 1912, and the slaughter of the First World War, which led inevitably to the victory of the Revolution. The Communists will never forgive Nicholas for the sins of his regime and, in their opinion, he deserved his fate.

On the day of his burial the Communists were lying low. They weren't even out on the Nevsky Prospekt, by Gostiny Dvor, where they distribute their propaganda every other day. Planned demonstrations did not materialize.

I made a few phone calls. There had been an archivist, a true Bolshevik, in the photographic archive around the corner where I had once worked many years ago. She and I had constant battles; she would insist there were no photographs of Trotsky during 1917 and deny that some later photograph had been doctored by the Soviet censors to exclude him. Olga Tikhonova couldn't be sure that she remembered me when I telephoned, but she said she'd be glad to receive me at her flat. It was small and dingy, with a portrait of Lenin in the hall, a copy of *Pravda* on the kitchen table, and the collected works of Stalin in a glass-fronted cabinet. She had retired, she was a pensioner, but she remembered me. Those battles of ours had been quite fierce.

Finally, we got to the subject of the Tsar. 'Lenin was correct, if the command came from him, to order the execution of the Tsar.' She had no doubts. 'It was necessary for the Revolution. Think how many more the White armies would have killed in the civil war if they thought it would have put the Tsar back on the throne.' She told me that her father had been shot by the Whites in Siberia when she was only a little girl. She did not remember him, and all she has ever had of his is a tiny photograph. She passed it to me in its frame, and I saw a serious young man in the uniform of a Red Army commissar. There seemed little point (not to mention taste) in trying to persuade her that none of the White leaders embraced monarchism as a cause, though there were many monarchists within their ranks. They all realized that it would be political suicide for them to support a restoration, since the Russian people had so utterly rejected the monarchy in February 1917. Kornilov was a republican (it was he who had arrested the Empress on 8 March) and widely detested (for this reason) by the monarchists; while Kolchak and Denikin (although themselves constitutional monarchists) proclaimed in their propaganda that they would allow a constituent assembly to decide the question of the state once the Bolsheviks had been overthrown. And that would have meant a republic.

But, I asked Olga, what about the daughters and the Tsarevich, the Empress and their servants who were also killed? Did they deserve to die? Olga had no reservations about the Empress: she had to be killed. More than eighty years after it had helped to bring down the Romanov regime, the myth of the 'German woman'—spying for the Kaiser and misruling Russia with her lover Rasputin—continued, it appeared, to dominate the revolutionary consciousness. Olga was also convinced that the Tsar's son had been a 'necessary murder' because 'otherwise he would have been a banner, a symbol of the restoration, not just for the Whites but for all the enemies of Soviet power who remained in the Soviet Union after the end of the civil war'. But when I pressed her on the daughters and the servants, she did not have a prepared argument. She thought for a while and then shrugged her shoulders: 'You must understand: it was a revolution.'

I left Olga's flat and went for a walk to clear my head. Outside the newly restored Cathedral of Christ's Resurrection with its brightly coloured onion domes there is a craft market where a busload of tourists were buying lacquer boxes and Russian dolls with the faces of the Tsars. This spot has become the perfect tourist trap—first the Cathedral, which was built in the fake medieval Russian style of the 1890s as part of the Tsar's hideous efforts to 'Muscovitize' St Petersburg; and then the Russian dolls, the *matrioshki*, which were invented during the same decade by the neo-nationalist artist, Sergei Maliutin. Tourists love this double dose of Romanov kitsch, thinking they are getting something of the 'real' (exotic) Russia that they had failed to find in the European city of St Petersburg. I saw stalls with ashtrays, cuff links, medals, knives and keyrings with the Romanov emblem of the double-headed eagle; icons and oil paintings of Nicholas II; and photographic histories of his reign. The funeral had attracted many Western tourists, especially from the United States. Most of them were second-generation Russian émigrés returning, as they said, to 'find their roots'. My plane from Helsinki had been full of them and I recognized some of them in the market. One gentleman from Wisconsin, who had told me on the plane that his great-uncle had been Prince Dolgorukov's manciple, was buying what the trader claimed to be a St George's Cross.

The posthumous cult of the Romanovs probably reached its height in 1991, when for many Russians a nostalgic view of the monarchy filled the ideological vacuum left by the collapse of the Soviet regime. It was in that year that Boris Yeltsin invited Vladimir Kirillovich Romanov, father of the pretender to the throne, to St Petersburg, where he was greeted by a crowd of 60,000 people. It was then, according to a poll, that about a fifth of the population supported the idea of a restoration of the monarchy. And it was then that the playwright, Edvard Radzinsky, published his *The Last Tsar: The Life and Death of Nicholas II*, a highly dramatized and sentimental account which became a best-seller. After that, interest dwindled as the Russians struggled to cope with the economic crises of the early Chernomyrdin years and began to realize that there was no easy return to the 'Russia we have lost' (the name of another best-seller from that time). By 1995, only seven per cent of the Russian people favoured the return of the monarchy. Now, three years later, interest in the idea seemed to have revived, encouraged by the increasingly nationalist rhetoric of the Orthodox Church, sections of the Duma, Yeltsin and his media. The most recent poll, published in the build-up to the funeral, suggested that about twelve per cent of the population favoured a constitutional monarchy.

For the Orthodox, Nicholas is no less than a saint. The Commission of the Holy Synod elected him to sainthood in 1996, and he and his family will be canonized in 2000, according to Father Georgy Mitrofan, who sits on the commission. I met Mitrofan the next day on the steps of St Isaac's Cathedral, just across from my hotel, and we walked together through the Alexander Gardens towards Palace Square. Plump and beady-eyed, like a cartoon parish priest, Father Georgy is a history graduate, yet he preached the

Church view on Russian history as if it were a doctrine beyond dispute. He explained to me how the Holy Synod's Commission decided on the holy status of the Tsar: 'Nicholas lived a holy life— one only has to read his diaries to see that. He did a great deal for the Church, and the Russian people loved and worshipped him. That is all he needs to become a saint.'

We stopped to have a beer from a booth with plastic chairs which called itself pretentiously the 'Café Palace Royale'. The Church, the priest told me, admitted that the Tsar had made some mistakes— Rasputin, for example—but it didn't regard them as sins. What about the Bloody Sunday massacre, which took place on the Palace Square in front of us, when several hundred peaceful demonstrators, led by the priest Gapon, were killed by Tsarist troops? 'That was not a peaceful demonstration,' Father Georgy said. 'It was a provocation, a mass armed demonstration, in itself a sin. Nicholas did not order the shooting. He wasn't even in the capital. Maybe he was responsible, but he was not to blame.' As for the pogroms against the Jews—which Nicholas applauded as the work of his 'loyal subjects' because, as he put it in a letter to his mother, 'nine-tenths of the troublemakers [i.e. the revolutionaries] are Jews'—the Tsar, it seemed, was also not to blame. It didn't seem worth pressing Mitrofan on the question of the Beilis Trial, in which it was later proved that Nicholas and his Minister of Justice had conspired to convict a Jew called Mendel Beilis for the ritual murder of a Christian boy, though they both knew that he was innocent, to demonstrate the general principle that such murders were committed by the Jews.

I asked instead why the Patriarch had not come to St Petersburg for the funeral. There had been much talk, stimulated by the possibility of his presence, of the role the Church might play in bringing about some sort of national reconciliation. But in the end he had gone instead to Zagorsk for a religious ceremony to commemorate the Tsar's death, and the St Petersburg funeral was purely a state affair. Georgy explained, in painstaking detail, that the Patriarch was not convinced that the bones were really those of the Romanovs. The Church did not recognize the scientific methods by which they had been tested and certified. The clergy had different standards of proof from DNA: miracles. No miracle had been connected with these relics, and without miracles it was hard for the Church to decide that these were the bones of a man whom it had decided to declare a saint. Georgy told me that many, if not most, of the clergy believed the ritual-murder theory, according to which the Tsar and his family were beheaded by the Jews and their corpses mutilated. Further proof that these were not the bones, because they show no signs of ritual murder. Father Georgy (who, it seemed to me, was much too sensible to believe such nonsense) tried to reassure me that the Holy Synod had ruled out this theory, but he was forced to admit that the Patriarch had been less than critical of those right-wing priests who had declared their belief in it.

The Church has not been in a conciliatory mood. It has given the impression that it is still fighting its own civil war, a campaign of revenge against its political and religious enemies. Its policy towards the Communists has continued to be based on the pastoral letter written in 1918 by Patriarch Tikhon in response to the Bolshevik Decree on the Separation of Church and State, in which the Patriarch anathematized the Bolsheviks as 'monsters of the human race'. Eighty years on, Father Georgy held the same view. 'There can be no place for Communists in a Christian or civilized society. Let them go and live in Siberia.' For a man of God, he sounded rather unforgiving. 'I bitterly regret that there was no proper trial of the Communist Party after 1991. In 1916 there were 146,000 clergy in Russia. By 1941 the Communists had shot 130,000 of them. Nothing like that has ever happened anywhere else. When people say that the Communists today are different from the Communists of those days, and that such things could not happen again, I know that it is just a lie.' The priest talked about the need to rebuild Russia on the basis of its national traditions, by which he meant the values of the Orthodox Church and the restoration of a monarchy, but he said he saw no point in trying to convert the Communists to these national ideals. When I asked about 'reconciliation', he got angry. There could be no reconciliation with the Communists, he said. 'The Communists have never repented for their sins. Frankly, all this talk of reconciliation is just Yeltsin and the others making capital.'

Later, that evening, I went to see Nikolai Braun, leader of the ultra-monarchist Union of Orders, who lives (ironically) on Lenin Street across the river. He was waiting for me on the pavement outside his home as my taxi (a real one) pulled up. He greeted me as if I were an old friend or ally of his cause—and at once I realized that he was a fanatic. 'I have brought along my archive,' he said referring to three large albums tucked under his arm. 'Let's go to a little place I know, and I will tell you all about our organization.' It sounded sinister. We sat down in a small café where MTV was blaring out on a huge set above our heads. First he showed me—as if to establish his credentials as a would-be national leader—letters of support from the Grand Duke Nikolai, head of the Romanov family, the Patriarch Alexei, and from various minor royals from around the globe. There was one from Prince Michael of Kent.

Braun spent ten years in Soviet jails as a dissident and there developed his militant brand of monarchism. He hated Communists. 'I could believe in a wolf atoning but not a Communist,' he told me in a phrase that I sensed he must have used often. 'Politicians like Yeltsin speak of the need for national reconciliation but there can be none as long as there are Communists.' This was the same language of civil war that I had already heard from Father Georgy. Braun too wanted a massive trial, a show trial of the Party, after 1991. 'They murdered 140 million people, eighty million during peacetime and sixty million during wars,' he declared, as if this breakdown of his preposterous statistic made it any more believable. 'It was the greatest crime in history—and no one has been punished.' By this stage Braun was carried away by his own rhetoric and was saying more than he perhaps should have said to a complete stranger. He suggested that 'perhaps a million' Communists should be sent to prison camps—and then added, as if to reassure me, 'as an example, you understand'. I raised my questions as politely as I could (as if they were minor problems of practicality). How would he decide which Communists to punish? Just the KGB and the Party leaders before 1991? Would that include Yeltsin (of whom he approves)? Or the rank and file as well? Just those who are still Communists, or also those who've left the Party? And, if the latter, when? He looked confused and paused for a moment. Simply Red were playing on MTV. Then his eyes lit up again: 'We could ship them all off to the

Arctic Circle where they can have their own little bits of land and settlements. Let them have their Leninist slogans there. Let them try out their experiments there.' A Gulag for the Communists.

This is a country where the scars of history are still too open to be healed. History is the obstacle to national unity; but understanding history, looking at it more objectively and accepting it as past, is surely the solution. Russians need to come to terms with all their history—the Communists with the Tsarist past, the monarchists with the Soviet—if they are to live in peace together as a nation. The trouble is that both sides—Red and White—are sustained by their own historical myths: the Reds by the myth that everything was dark in Tsarist Russia; the Whites by the myth that everything was light. And vice versa.

The White myth dominated the media's coverage of the funeral. Anything approaching an objective view of the historical role of Nicholas was not to be seen on the television. He was presented, together with his lovely daughters, as the innocent victim of a barbaric revolution—as if his own policies and attitudes had nothing to do with its cause. What might have been a day of national mourning for *all* the victims of the Terror had been hijacked by television as a purely monarchist event, with all the nation's grief focused on the royal coffins, Diana-style. Television pictures from the ceremony were intercut with photographs of the Tsar and his family on happy picnics and boating trips in some summer before the First World War. A Chopin prelude played in the background, and the commentator told us (as if he knew): 'What a wonderful family it was! How beautiful and graceful were the Grand Duchesses! All so soon to be senselessly destroyed!'

Legends, nostalgia: and at the heart of them a yearning for the bourgeois family ideal, for the genteel and decent life the Romanovs enjoyed but the common Russian people never had. As my old acquaintance, Vitaly Startsev, sometime Professor of History at the Herzen Institute, explained over coffee when I visited him at his apartment the following morning: 'People do not know their history. They look at Nicholas and see a charming man who loved his family and was kind to everyone. These are qualities which they never saw in their Soviet leaders—and so they conclude that the Tsarist government was, or must have been, more humane as well.'

And so the media peddled the idea of Tsarist Russia as a lost idyll. 'Russia was embarking on a period of greatness and well being in 1913,' Valery Ostrovsky told his viewers, as they watched (again) those lovely scenes of the Tsar and his daughters dancing on the deck of the imperial yacht. 'The rouble, which today is the weakest in the world, was then one of the strongest currencies.' Ostrovsky is a well-known television don, a historian young and bright enough not to have been corrupted by the old Soviet system. Under Gorbachev he ' used to preach the liberal virtues of democracy. But throughout this coverage he spoke the language of a monarchist. 'Nicholas was one of the world's most important statesmen. He was a great patriot and thought only of Russia and the people. He gave them freedom and the people enjoyed freedom and loved their Tsar.'

Even Dmitry Likhachev, who is perhaps the most respected voice of the nation's liberal consciousness, was not immune. Likhachev, at ninety-two, has lived through Russia's century of terror and upheaval. He has always been a figure above politics, a spokesman for the humanist ideals towards which the Westernist intelligentsia in Russia has always aspired. His books on Russia's cultural history have been read by millions; he has been enormously influential. Yet in those days of the funeral he too showed his political colours. 'The Revolution,' he said on television, 'was simply a nightmare. When the Tsar was murdered it felt as if the sun had left the world. This was the end of a relatively humanitarian period in Russian history and the start of a new barbarian epoch.'

No serious effort, then, to explain the Revolution and Nicholas's role in bringing it about. Almost nothing about his lack of talent as a politician—of his rigid adherence to the archaic vision of autocracy which he inherited from his father; nothing of his refusal to face up to the new social forces of capitalist and industrial Russia; nothing of his contempt for liberalism and the rule of law; or of his obstinate unwillingness to delegate his powers to able ministers, such as Witte or Stolypin, who alone had projects of reform that might, just might, have saved his dynasty. And nothing, or nothing much, about his adamant refusal (once the danger of the 1905 revolution had been dealt with) to grant more freedoms to the new parliamentary parties, or to local government and trade unions, the effect of which was to force these potentially loyal elements into the revolutionary underground and to direct it towards violent extremes. This was a man who did not have the wits to understand the challenge of his reign, a man who devoted all his energies to the minutiae of his autocratic office (even sealing envelopes with his own gentle hand) as a catastrophe gathered outside his door. Indeed, he barely seemed aware of it as he retreated more and more from public life and took refuge in the private and equally damaged realm of his family. While Petrograd sank into chaos, he wrote in his diary on 26 February 1917: 'At ten o'clock I went to mass. The reports were on time. There were many people at breakfast. Wrote to Alix and went for a walk near the chapel by the Bobrinsky road. The weather was fine and frosty. After tea I read and talked with Senator Tregubov until dinner. Played dominoes in the evening.' The next morning he lost his throne.

The media coverage of his funeral, eighty-one years later, presented his overthrow as the first cause of the terrible events that came after: the October Revolution in the same year, the anarchy and terror of the Bolshevik regime (with the Tsar and his family among the dead), and onwards through Stalin to Brezhnev. The Revolution by this interpretation was a crime, a senseless wave of barbaric violence led by a small clique of criminals and terrorists. 'We were all guilty,' Yeltsin proclaimed. 'We behaved so badly,' Ostrovsky said, 'that we should all now bow our heads in shame. The whole Revolution was nothing more than a criminal adventure.' Yury Gergin, another historian, told the audience of Channel 6: 'Nicholas was the last legitimate ruler of the country until the election of President Yeltsin. All the others in between were criminal usurpers. The Revolution was illegal.' But then, by definition, revolutions are.

So much has been conveniently forgotten. When I pointed out to Braun, the monarchist, that there were about 300,000 people on the streets of Petrograd calling for the downfall of the Tsar, he quibbled at the figure. 'Even if there were, at most, 100,000 people, the authorities could have dealt with them. The police could have isolated them—the terrorists and the hooligans, not the honest people, you understand—in one sector of the city; and then they should have warned them that it was a sin to rise up against the Tsar. If they failed to disperse, the police should have fired at them.' There seemed no point in asking him: would this not have been a greater sin?

In any case, repression was impossible. The Tsar's own senior generals had told him this, and it had convinced him to abdicate. The 250,000 soldiers of the Petrograd garrison had gone over to the people's side on 27 February, forcing the police in the capital to flee. No armed force could have put down what became a national uprising against the monarchy, and even the Tsar's loyal supporters soon turned themselves in to the Revolution's leaders at the Tauride Palace rather than run the risk of the people's wrath. Huge crowds tore down Tsarist flags and emblems from public buildings and burned them in bonfires on the street. Tsarist statues and symbols were destroyed. Effigies of the Tsar were burned and the eyes cut out, voodoo-style, from monarchist portraits. People even called for the Empress to be killed, believing the rumours that she was a German spy. Indeed the overthrow of the Tsar was widely hailed as a patriotic act. As someone put it at the time: 'Now we have beaten the Germans here, we will beat them in the field.'

People of all classes—not just 'terrorists and hooligans'—joined the call for blood. Viktor Steklov, a distinguished mathematician, wrote in his diary on 10 March that the Tsar and his family were 'scum, not human beings...we should hang them all like worthless scum'. Steklov was a man of moderate views, a political liberal. Among the lower classes, who had greater cause to detest the monarchy, there were louder calls for retribution. There were frequent calls by workers and troops for the Tsar and his family to be shot. 'And they shouldn't spare the daughters' was a popular refrain. All of which confirms the old but long-forgotten Soviet claim (confirmed by the Patriarch of Moscow in his address to mark the eightieth anniversary of their deaths) that the news of their execution was received by the people with indifference.

There are times when every nation needs to think a little less about its history. Dwelling on the past can stop a people moving on. In St Petersburg, I saw that in some ways the Russian people needed to forget about their revolution. How are they to become united and prosper as a nation unless they forget their divisions of the past? It is their history that has crippled them. Russia in this way is like Ireland.

But I also saw how the Russians needed to learn their history, otherwise they would never overcome its legacies. As yet they remain ignorant of it. Most people know very little about Nicholas or any of the Tsars, since the subject was always poorly taught and grossly distorted in Soviet schools. There are just as many gaps in post-Tsarist, Soviet history. The result has been that myths and conspiracy theories are substituted for historical knowledge. Even some 'educated' Russians still believe that the February Revolution was a masonic plot; that the Empress was a German spy and the lover of Rasputin; that the Bolsheviks were controlled by the Germans (or the Jews); or that the Tsarevich, or Anastasia, miraculously managed to escape the firing squad and fled into the woods to live with nuns, or Siberian peasants, or were whisked away by the Whites to live in peace as private citizens in Mongolia, Canada or New Zealand. How many times have I been told by Russians that the Tsarevich survived? (I tell you, he did not.)

Ignorance and gullibility play into the hands of demagogues. Zhirinovsky, Lebed and Zyuganov—they all have their own pernicious myths of Russian history. The Communists will tell you that the Western powers are still sheltering the Romanovs so that, when the time is right, they can restore them to the throne. Nationalists such as Zhirinovsky say that Russia has been run by foreigners all along—the Germans before 1917, the Jews and Georgians afterwards, and now the capitalists of the West. Monarchist extremists believe that the Tsar was ritually murdered by the Jews, who have always conspired to ruin Russia, and that all Jews should be expelled from the country. Without some truer version of their past, one is forced to conclude that the Russians will never arrive at the destination of a liberal and tolerant democracy.

The immediate prospects are not encouraging. The Russians are fed up with their history. They are tired of the revelations that made glasnost so exciting, when nearly every day some new fact about their rulers appeared in the newspapers and on television. The 'new Russians' make and spend a lot of money—or at least they did before the August crash—but they have little time for history or books. The young, especially, who aspire to become fully Westernized, are hostile to the image of 'backwardness' which they associate with Russian history. They think about the future rather than the past; they enrol for courses in computer studies, English and business management, while history enrolments at universities are at an all-time low. The number of new academic history books published every year can be counted on two hands, and none sells more than about a thousand copies. The only grounds for optimism are the schools, where some decent history textbooks have at last replaced the Communist version of Russia's story.

St Petersburg airport was packed on the day I left. Everyone was getting out. The funeral had put the city on the world map for a few days; it had been the last hurrah for Russia's old imperial capital. Now the television crews were leaving. Standing next to me in the queue at customs was a young Russian woman who was on her way to England to study for A levels in economics and sociology. The queue was not moving—there was some trouble with a television crew that refused to put its cameras through the X-ray machines— and so we got to talking in a general way. Finally I asked her the question I'd been asking every Russian since the day I arrived. 'Oh them,' she said, 'they're just a pile of bones.' At first I was shocked, perhaps even a little disappointed, that an event of such significance for Russian history (and for my career) was of so little interest to her. But then it occurred to me that her indifference was also a hopeful sign that for her generation the whole bitter episode was in the distant past, that it had been buried like the bones. □

THE LOST BOYS
Anna Pyasetskaya
and Heidi Bradner

The war in Chechnya was the bloodiest event to come out of the break-up of
the Soviet Union. At least 50,000 people died—about a fifth of them
Russian soldiers, mostly young conscripts. Anna Pyasetskaya is a member of
the Committee of Soldiers' Mothers of Russia. The following account is of her
struggle to find her son. The pictures, by Heidi Bradner, show the Russian
army before it withdrew in defeat in the winter of 1996.

Anna Pyasetskaya

My son Nikolai Nikolaevich Pyasetsky—Kolya to his friends and family—was called up into the Russian army on 24 May 1994. He was twenty.

He went for training at the Special Air Force centre in Omsk and then to the Ryazan regiment of the Tula division of the Special Air Force. The base isn't far from our home in Moscow, and I was glad he would be so near. We spoke on the phone on 28 November. He promised to find out when it would be convenient to visit and asked me to arrange a telephone call to him on 4 December. This was my last conversation with my son. On the following day, 29 November, he was flown with the rest of his battalion to Chechnya, though I didn't discover this till much later.

On 22 December we learned—from unofficial sources—that Kolya had been sent for duty in a 'southerly direction'. We knew by then that Russian troops had invaded Chechnya. We immediately wrote to ask: where is our son?

From the newspapers I found out that the Committee of Soldiers' Mothers of Russia was collecting parcels for young men who had been sent to Chechnya. I went to their headquarters on 25 December. They took a parcel for my son. I still didn't know where he was. I found out the telephone number of his division headquarters and rang every day from 26 December to ask about him. I was always given the same answer: he is not among the dead and wounded. Then, on 5 January, I was told that my son Nikolai Pyasetsky had been killed in Grozny.

For five days I walked around like a shadow unable to eat or drink. I prayed to God for our boys, the thousands of them, who had died in the battle of New Year's Eve. I cried for them all.

It wasn't until 11 January, after the holidays had ended, that I was able to appeal to the Tula division for my son's body to be returned to me. They told me that my son had disappeared without trace. I rang the headquarters again and was told to wait. New information: 'all the bodies are being collected in Rostov-on-Don, and from there your son's body will be sent to Moscow'.

I rang military section No. 41450 again to ask how my son had died. I discovered that my Kolya was in personnel carrier No. 785 which had entered Grozny on 1 January. Of the twelve members of the crew only three remained alive. It wasn't clear what had happened;

the vehicle had not been found. I managed to contact one of the survivors, Seryozha Rodionov. He was recovering from his wounds in Novocherkassk hospital. He said that my Kolya had been killed inside the vehicle close to the railway station. The Russian soldiers did not know the town: they had no maps. On 25 January I discovered that the vehicle had been found but that the body of my son was not in it.

On 26 January I flew with a group from the BBC a thousand miles south to the town of Nazran in Ingushetia, the state which borders Chechnya. Thousands of refugees had gathered in the town, and hundreds of mothers had come from all over Russia to look for their sons, though only a few managed to find them alive. On the first day in Nazran I discovered that a Chechen woman who conveyed the wounded from Grozny to Stariye Atagi had Kolya's military card. I wanted to find her and see if she knew anything of my son and so I went to Grozny. In the basement of city hospital No. 2 I met Maria Ivanovna Kirbasova, the chairperson of the Committee of Soldier's Mothers of Russia. I learned from her that my Kolya was not on the list of prisoners.

Planes bombed the town every day and there was constant shooting. I was not afraid, I just wanted to know the fate of my son. I didn't manage to track down the Chechen woman until 31 January. She was called Zarema. She gave me my son's military card but couldn't tell me how or where she had come across it. The thread was broken. I went back to Nazran, but did not stay long.

I decided to try to discover more from the military headquarters in Beslan and then to travel to Rostov-on-Don where they were collecting the bodies of dead soldiers. At the headquarters they told me that my son's body must be in Rostov. I flew north to Rostov early in the morning of 2 February and looked through the books where the names of dead soldiers were registered. My Kolya was not on any of the lists. I was told that only forty per cent of the bodies had been identified. I had to look through all the railway carriages filled with dead bodies. I will never be able to forget this horror.

The carriages were packed full. Many bodies were already unrecognizable: bitten by dogs, cut into pieces, burned… A month had already passed since the start of the war. Rostov was simply unable to cope. Apart from the train carriages, there was also a tent city near the hospital. The tents were also packed with bodies. I went through all the carriages and tents looking at every boy, the faces, the hair, and if there was no head, the hands and feet. My Kolya would be easy to find, he had a birthmark on his right cheek. There were some other mothers with me. One of them recognized her son, but I was not able to find Kolya. The soldiers told me that not all the carriages were in Rostov—there were more in Mozdok, close to the Chechen border. So I went south again to Mozdok, to the 'Mir' cinema. Hundreds of mothers gathered here every day. Each one was trying to find her son.

I needed to look through the carriages of dead bodies which had come from Grozny to Mozdok. I approached an officer who said he would help me, but the next time we met he said he could do nothing. 'What do you expect to be able to achieve? Your son is listed missing without trace.' I was overcome with despair.

Again I went to Grozny. Together with a young Japanese journalist I visited the cemetery where corpses from the whole town had been assembled: men, women, Christians, Muslims, all made equal in death. I did not find my son. Now, despairing of finding his body, I decided to look for him alive. I thought that in the mystery of God's plan he might have been taken prisoner.

On 4 April a group of us from the Soldiers' Mothers of Russia went to the village of Vedeno, the headquarters of Aslan Maskhadov, the Chechen leader. Each woman had made her own way there. There were twenty-two of us and we met up at the Chechen military headquarters. The Chechens are a hospitable people and all the women were offered overnight accommodation. Three other Russian mothers, Svetlana Belikova, Tanya Ivanova, Olya Osipenko and I were put up in a flat whose inhabitants had gone to Voronezh. We lived for almost two months in Vedeno, periodically going to mountain villages to look for our children.

Day followed day. In May there came a splinter of hope. We heard that some of the prisoners were in the mountains of Shatoi and my son's surname was mentioned. On 5 May we were received by Aslan Maskhadov. A ceasefire had been negotiated but the Russians had not fulfilled their obligations: the exchange of prisoners could not take place. The front got closer and closer to Vedeno, Russian bombing raids became frequent, and seven times the village was hit. One bomb reduced a two-storey building to rubble and it took three days to dig out the dead. There were eleven of them, mainly women and children. We were seized by despair. We were Russians, the bombs were Russian bombs. Can people who sit in aeroplanes and deliver death be called human beings? A few mornings later we experienced the full horror of bombing for ourselves. The planes came suddenly as we were sitting down at the table for breakfast. The first bomb exploded thirty metres away. The windows blew out. As we ran towards the door, a second bomb hit the corner of our house. The floor above us collapsed, doors were wrenched off their hinges, the air was filled with dust and flying glass. We hid in the basement for the next half-hour until the raid ended. We were lucky. Sveta [Svetlana] had been lacerated by the glass, her leg swelled up and she found it difficult to walk, but the rest of us were unhurt.

We stayed on in Vedeno for a few days after the bombing. The bazaar was closed, it was impossible to buy food, and, because our house was destroyed, we had to sleep in the open. The sky was starry and the planes flew across it with their signal-lights on. Against the background of the stars it was difficult to make them out and they bombed with no fear that they would be hit by fire from the ground. I often recall those nights. We lay down under a blanket and tried to distinguish the planes from the stars. If a star began to fall it meant that a plane was preparing to bomb.

I thought that only the love of a person for all that lives could stop this madness.

We sent Olya with Sveta to another village where it was less dangerous, and then Tanya and I managed to persuade the Chechen fighters to take us with them into the Shatoi mountains where we thought our children might be. It was a tough journey along mountain paths, moving only at night without any lights or torches because planes were always in the sky. For two months we went from village to village. The fighters helped as much as they could, sharing their bread and distributing details of our children. We were bombed and fired upon several times. But we did not find our sons.

We headed back to Grozny along a road which was littered with burned and abandoned Russian vehicles and hundreds of dead

Russian soldiers. There were many mass graves by the roadside. It was impossible to see all this without tears.

In Grozny I met some Chechen women whom I'd got to know on my previous visit, and we exchanged information. But there was nothing they could say to encourage our hope. I felt it was time to go home to Moscow—I'd been looking for my son now for seven months. Tanya decided to stay and continue looking for her son Andrei. I left Kolya's photo with her.

I reached Moscow on 20 August and on 4 September Tanya rang: she had recognized my Kolya from a video made on 21 February. Under the name Yevgeny Sergeyevich Gilev he had been buried 2,000 miles east of Moscow, in the Altai Mountains in a village called Stepnoe Ozero. Yevgeny's parents had opened the coffin when it arrived in their village but it was no longer possible to recognize the body. So they buried my son instead of their own. Six months later they buried another person; this time it was their son. He had been in carriage No. 162; his name was hidden in a pendant. His mother came to Rostov and recognized him and took him home. They buried him not far from my Kolya. The two lay together for a while until, on 15 October, my son was dug up and taken to Moscow, where I had requested that he be reburied.

Tanya Ivanova came to the funeral. In Rostov she had identified her Andrei, although the word 'identify' is not appropriate. He was completely burned: experts named him after taking X-rays of his skull and his chest and determining his blood group. Tanya had just buried her only son, but still she came to my son's funeral and responded to my grief. I am very grateful.

And how did the army help? Not at all. Only one person from my son's unit came to the funeral. The coffin was carried not by paratroopers but by my son's school friends. I was told there would be no government funding for the funeral because there were so many dead. And yet in his next breath the man who told me this, the representative of military unit No. 41450, spoke about the call of duty which my son had obeyed.

What is this debt? What do we owe this state which has taken from me my most precious thing? ☐

Translation by Patricia Cocrell and Galina Orlova

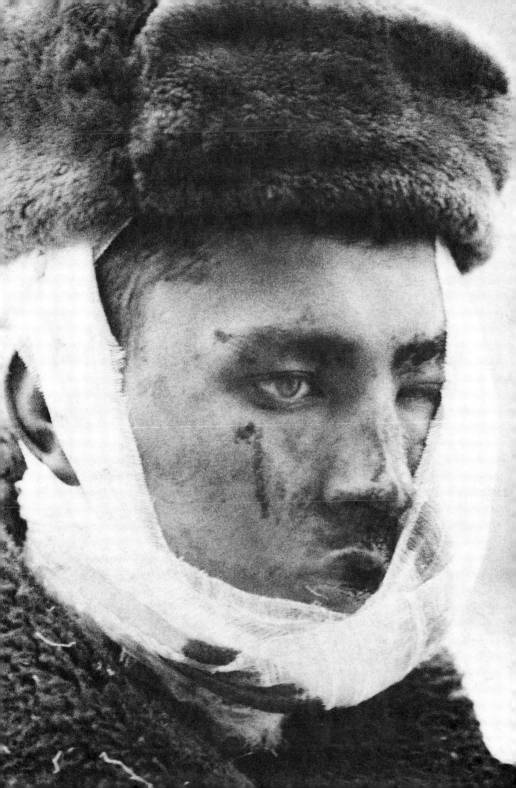

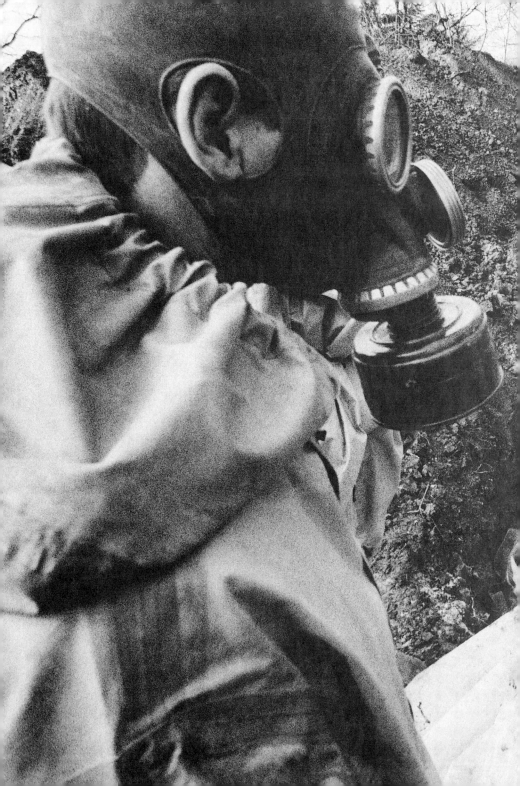

THE RIVER POTUDAN
Andrei Platonov

TRANSLATION BY ROBERT AND ELIZABETH
CHANDLER AND ANGELA LIVINGSTONE

Grass had grown back on the trodden-down dirt tracks of the civil war, because the war had stopped. With peace the provinces had grown quiet again and there were fewer people: some had died in the fighting, many were being treated for their wounds and were resting with their families, forgetting the heavy work of the war in long sleep. Demobilized men in old greatcoats were still making their way home, carrying kitbags and wearing helmets or sheepskin caps—walking over the thick unfamiliar grass which there had not been time to see before, or maybe it had just been trampled down by the campaigns and had not been growing then. They walked with faint, astonished hearts, recognizing afresh the fields and villages that lay along their path. Their souls had been changed by the torment of war, by illness and the happiness of victory, and it was as if they were approaching life for the first time, dimly remembering themselves as they had been three or four years ago. They were older and had grown up, they had become wiser and more patient and had started to feel inside themselves the great universal hope which had become the idea of their lives—lives that were still young and which, before the civil war, had had no clear aim or purpose.

In the late summer of 1921 the last demobilized Red Army soldiers were dispersing. They had been kept back on the labour teams, working at unfamiliar trades, feeling homesick; only now had they been told to go home to their own lives and to life in general.

A former Red Army soldier, Nikita Firsov, on his way home to an obscure provincial town, had been walking for more than a day now along a ridge that stretched beside the River Potudan. Nearly twenty-five years had passed since this man's birth, and he had a modest face that seemed permanently sorrowful—though this expression may have been caused not by sadness but by some restrained goodness of character or, perhaps, simply the intensity of youth. From under his cap his fair hair, which had not been cut for a long time, hung down to his ears, and his large grey eyes gazed anxiously at the monotonous landscape, as if the man on foot were not from these parts.

At noon Nikita Firsov lay down beside a small stream that flowed along the bottom of a gully and down into the Potudan. He dozed off on the earth, under the sun, in September grass that had become tired of growing there ever since the distant spring. Life's warmth seemed to go dark in him as he fell asleep in the quiet of this remote place. Insects flew past his face, a spider's web floated above him; a tramp stepped over the sleeping man, neither touching him nor curious at all, and continued on his way. The dust of the summer and the long drought stood high in the air, dimming the light of the sky, but still the world's time went on as usual, following the sun in its course. Suddenly Firsov sat up, breathing heavily and fearfully, as though he were on fire, winded from some invisible race and struggle. He had had a terrible dream—that a small plump animal was suffocating him with its hot fur, some sort of field creature grown fat from eating pure wheat. Soaking with sweat from its effort and greed, this creature had got into the sleeper's mouth, into his throat, trying to burrow with its tenacious little paws into the very centre of his soul, burning up his breath. Firsov had choked in his sleep and had wanted to cry out, but the small creature had torn itself out of him of its own accord, blind, pitiful, itself terrified and trembling, and had vanished in the darkness of its night.

Firsov washed in the stream and rinsed out his mouth, then walked on quickly; his father's house was not far away now and he could get there by evening.

Just as it grew dark Firsov caught sight of his birthplace. It was a gently sloping upland which rose from the banks of the Potudan to some high fields of rye. There was a little town on this upland, now almost invisible because of the darkness. Not a single light was burning.

Nikita Firsov's father was asleep; he had gone to bed as soon as he got home from work, before the sun had set. He lived alone. His wife was long dead and two of his sons had disappeared during the imperialist war. The last son, Nikita, might yet come back, thought the father; the civil war wasn't so far away—outside people's houses, in their yards—and there was less shooting than in the imperialist one. The father slept a lot—from dusk till dawn; if he didn't sleep, he began to think and remember, and his heart ached with longing for his lost sons, and with sorrow for his life that had passed by so dismally. As soon as morning came he went off to the furniture workshop where he had worked as a joiner for many years now—and there in the midst of work everything became more bearable and he forgot himself. But towards evening his soul felt worse again; returning home to his one room, he would go to sleep quickly, almost in a panic, until the next day; he did not even need any paraffin. But at dawn the fleas would start biting his bald patch and the old man would wake and, little by little, would carefully dress himself, put his shoes on, wash and sigh and stamp about, tidy the room, mutter to himself, go outdoors to look at the weather, then come back in—anything to while away the useless time that remained before work began.

That night Nikita Firsov's father was sleeping as usual. A cricket had lived for years in the earth ledge outside the house and it used to sing there in the evenings: it was either the same cricket as the summer before last or else its grandson. Nikita went up to the ledge and knocked on his father's small window; the cricket fell silent for a moment as if trying to make out who this could be—a strange man arriving so late. The father got down from the old wooden bed he had slept on with the mother of all his sons; Nikita himself had been born on that very bed. The thin old man was in his underpants; they had shrunk from years of wear and washing, and now they only reached to his knees. The father leaned right up against the window pane and looked out at his son. He had already seen him and recognized him, but still he went on looking, wanting to look his fill. Then he ran out of the door and through the yard, short and skinny as a boy, to open the wicket-gate which had been bolted for the night.

Nikita entered the old room, with its sleeping-bench, its low ceiling and its one small window on to the street. It still smelled the same as it had in his childhood, the same as three years ago when he had left for the war; even the smell of his mother's skirt was still here—here and nowhere else in the world. Nikita put down his bag and cap, slowly took off his coat, and sat on the bed. His father remained standing in front of him, barefoot, in his underpants, not daring to greet him properly or to start talking.

'Well?' he asked after a while. 'What's happened to those bourgeois and Kadets? Are there any left, or did you finish them all off?'

'Not quite,' said his son, 'but we got nearly all of them.'

The father pondered this intently for a moment: they had killed off a whole class—quite an achievement.

'Well, they always were a spineless lot,' the old man said of the bourgeois. 'What use have they ever been? They've always lived off the backs of others.'

Nikita stood up in front of his father; he was now a whole head and a half taller than him. Facing his son the old man was silent in the humble bewilderment of his love for him. Nikita laid a hand on his father's head and drew him to his breast. The old man leaned against his son and began to breathe deeply and fast, as if he had reached his resting place.

On one of the streets of the town, which ran straight out into a field, stood a wooden house with green shutters. An old widow, a teacher at the town school, had once lived in this house and her children had lived with her—a son about ten years old, and a fifteen-year-old daughter, a fair-haired girl called Lyuba.

A few years ago, Nikita Firsov's father had wanted to marry the widowed schoolteacher, but he had soon given the idea up. Twice, when Nikita was still a boy, his father had taken him to visit the teacher, and Nikita had seen Lyuba there, a thoughtful girl who sat reading books, paying no attention to these strangers who had come as her mother's guests.

The old schoolteacher had treated the joiner to tea and rusks and spoken about enlightening the minds of the people and repairing the school stoves. Nikita's father sat silent throughout; he was embarrassed, he grunted and coughed and smoked home-made cigarettes, then timidly sipped tea from the saucer, not touching the rusks, as if he were already full.

There had been chairs in the schoolteacher's home, in both of the two rooms and in the kitchen, and there had been curtains at the windows; in the first room stood a piano and a clothes cupboard, and in the second room there were beds and two soft armchairs of red velvet, as well as a lot of books on the shelves along the wall. The father and son had found all this too wealthy and the father had stopped going to see her after the second visit. He had not even managed to tell her that he wanted to marry her. But Nikita had been curious to see the piano again and the thoughtful girl who was always reading, and he had asked his father to propose to the old woman, so they could go on visiting her.

'I can't, Nikit,' his father had said. 'I'm not educated enough, what would I talk to her about? And I'd be ashamed to ask them to our place: we've got no cups and saucers and our food isn't good enough. Did you see the armchairs they had? Antiques, from Moscow! And the cupboard? Carving and fretwork all over the front—I know about that sort of thing! And as for the daughter! She'll probably go to college.'

And now it was some years since the father had seen his old intended bride, though there had been times, perhaps, when he had missed her or at least had thought about her.

The day after he got home from the civil war Nikita went to the Military Commissariat to register for the reserve. Then he walked around the familiar, beloved town where he had been born, and his heart began to ache to see the small houses grown old, the rotting fences of wood and wattle, the few apple trees left in the yards, many already dead and dried up for ever. In his childhood the apple trees had been green, and the one-storey houses had seemed large and wealthy, inhabited by mysterious, clever people; the streets had been long, the burdock leaves tall, and the plants had grown wild on patches of wasteland, and in neglected kitchen plots, like sinister copses and thickets. Now Nikita saw that the small houses were low and wretched, in need of paint and repair, that the tall weeds on the wasteland were pathetic, more dejected than terrifying, lived in only by old, patient ants, and that the streets soon came to an end in the earth of the fields and the light space of the sky. The town had shrunk. Nikita thought it must mean he had lived through a lot of his life, if large mysterious objects had now become small and dull.

He walked slowly past the house with green shutters, where once he had gone visiting with his father. The green paint was just a memory—only faint traces of it remained. It had faded in the sun, been washed off by rain, or had flaked away down to the wood. The iron roof on the house had grown rusty—rain probably came through these days and the ceiling above the piano would be damp. Nikita looked attentively through the windows of the house: there were no curtains now and on the other side of the panes was somebody else's unfamiliar darkness. Nikita sat down on a bench by the wicket-gate of the decayed, though still familiar, house. He half expected someone inside to start playing the piano, then he would listen to music. But the house remained silent, giving nothing away. After waiting a little, Nikita looked into the yard through a crack in the fence: there were great clumps of old nettles, a bare path running between them to a shed, and three wooden steps leading up to the front door. The old teacher and her daughter Lyuba must have died long ago and the little boy would have gone to the war as a volunteer...

Nikita set off for home. It was getting towards evening; his father would soon be back for the night, and they would need to think about how he was to live and where he should go for work.

On the main street people were taking their evening stroll; the town had begun to come back to life now that the war was over. The street was full of office clerks, girl students, soldiers who had been demobilized or who were recovering from their wounds, youngsters, people who worked at home or in their own workshops; the factory workers came out later, when it was dark. People were shabbily dressed, in old clothes or in worn-out army uniforms from imperialist times.

Nearly everyone who passed Nikita by, even the couples walking arm in arm, was carrying something for their household. The women carried potatoes, or sometimes fish, in home-made bags, while the men held a ration of bread or half a cow's head under their arms, and some were cupping their hands protectively round pieces of offal which would be made into soup. But hardly anyone looked miserable, only the occasional exhausted old man. Most of the younger people were laughing, looking closely into each other's faces, animated and trustful, as if on the eve of eternal happiness.

'Hello!' a woman said to Nikita timidly, from a little way off.

Her voice immediately touched and warmed him, as if someone beloved and lost were answering his call for help. Yet it seemed to Nikita that he must be mistaken and that the greeting was for somebody else. But when Nikita stopped and looked behind him he saw Lyuba: a big, grown-up Lyuba who was looking at him with a sad, embarrassed smile.

Nikita went up to her and looked at her carefully, for she had been precious to him even in memory: had all of her truly been preserved? Her Austrian shoes, tied up with string, were worn right down, her pale muslin dress reached only to her knees—there had probably not been enough cloth for a longer skirt—and this dress immediately made Nikita feel sorry for Lyuba: he had seen dresses like it on women in their coffins, yet here the muslin covered a body that was alive and full-grown, only very poor. Over the dress was an old jacket—Lyuba's mother must have worn it as a girl—and her head was uncovered; she wore her hair in a bright, firm plait coiled at the nape of her neck.

'Don't you remember me?' asked Lyuba.

'Yes, I do,' answered Nikita. 'I haven't forgotten you.'

'One should never forget,' smiled Lyuba.

Her pure eyes looked tenderly at Nikita as if admiring him. Nikita looked into her face in return, and the mere sight of her eyes, sunk deep from the hardships of life but illumined by trust and hope, made his heart feel both joy and pain.

Nikita and Lyuba walked back to her house—she still lived in the same place. Her mother had died not so long ago, and her younger brother had been fed at a Red Army field kitchen during the famine and had got so used to life there that he had gone off south with the soldiers to fight the enemy.

'He got used to eating *kasha* there,' said Lyuba, 'and there wasn't any at home.'

Lyuba now lived in one room—it was all she needed. With numbed feelings, Nikita looked round this room where he had seen Lyuba and the piano and all the costly furnishings for the first time. There was no piano now, no cupboard with fretwork over its front; only the two upholstered armchairs remained, and a table and a bed. The wallpaper was faded and torn, the floor was worn down, and beside the tiled stove stood a smaller iron stove which you could heat with a handful of wood-shavings so as to warm yourself a little.

Lyuba pulled out a thick notebook from under her blouse, then took off her shoes. She was now a student at the district academy of medical science. In those years there were universities and academies everywhere because the people wanted to fill themselves with knowledge as quickly as possible. The human heart had been tormented too much, not only by hunger and poverty but by the meaninglessness of life, and now they needed to understand what human existence really was: was it something serious or was it a joke?

'My shoes hurt me,' said Lyuba. 'Sit there for a while, and I'll lie down and have a sleep. I'm terribly hungry and I don't want to have to think about it.'

Without undressing, she slipped underneath the blanket that was on the bed and laid her plait over her eyes.

Nikita sat silently for two or three hours, until Lyuba woke and got up. It was night by then, and dark in the room.

'I don't suppose my friend will come today,' she said sadly.

'Do you need her then?' asked Nikita.

'Yes, very much,' said Lyuba. 'They're a large family and her father's in the army. If there's any leftovers she brings me supper—first I eat, and then we get down to our studies together.'

'Do you have any paraffin?'

'No, I've been given some firewood. We light the little stove—then we sit on the floor. We can see by the flame.'

Lyuba smiled helplessly, with shame, as if some cruel, sad thought had entered her mind.

'I expect her elder brother is still awake,' she said. 'He's just a lad. He doesn't like his sister feeding me, he begrudges it. But it isn't my fault! I'm really not all that fond of eating. It's not me—it's my head. It starts aching and thinking about bread, it stops me from living and thinking about anything else.'

'Lyuba!' a youthful voice called out near the window.

'Zhenya!' Lyuba called back.

Lyuba's friend came in. She took four large baked potatoes from her pocket and put them on the iron stove.

'Did you get the Histology?' asked Lyuba.

'Who would I get it from?' answered Zhenya. 'They've put my name down for it at the library.'

'Never mind, we'll get by,' said Lyuba. 'I learned the first two chapters by heart at the academy. I'll say it and you write it down. Will that work?'

'It's worked before!' Zhenya said with a laugh.

Nikita got the stove going so the fire would give them light for their notebooks, then got ready to return to his father's for the night.

'You won't forget me now?' Lyuba asked as she said goodbye.

'No,' said Nikita, 'I've no one else to remember.'

Nikita rested at home for two days, and then started work at the furniture workshop where his father was employed. He was taken on as a carpenter, to work on the preparation of materials, and his wage was lower than his father's, almost twice as low. But Nikita knew that after he learned his trade he would be promoted to joiner and his pay would be better.

Nikita had never lost the habit of work. In the Red Army they had done other things besides fighting; during long halts, or while they were held in reserve, they had dug wells, repaired the huts of poor peasants, and planted bushes at the tops of ravines to prevent more earth being washed away. The war would come to an end, but life would go on, and it needed to be thought about in advance.

A week later Nikita went to visit Lyuba again, taking her a present of some boiled fish and bread—the main course of his dinner at the workers' canteen.

Lyuba was at the window, hurrying to get her reading done before the sun left the sky, so Nikita sat silently in Lyuba's room for some time, waiting for the darkness of night. Soon the twilight matched the silence of the provincial street, and Lyuba rubbed her eyes and closed her textbook.

'How are you?' Lyuba asked quietly.

'My father and I are all right, we're alive,' said Nikita. 'I've got something here for you. Please eat it,' he begged.

'I will,' said Lyuba. 'Thank you.'

'You won't be going to sleep?' asked Nikita.

'No,' answered Lyuba, 'I'm having supper now, so I'll be full!'

Nikita brought some kindling from the entrance and lit the iron stove so there would be light to study by. He sat down on the floor, opened the stove door and put some chips of wood and small logs on the fire, trying to make it give more light. After eating the fish and bread, Lyuba sat down on the floor too, opposite Nikita and beside the light from the stove, and began studying medicine from her book.

She read silently, but from time to time she would whisper something, smile, and write down more words in her notebook in small quick handwriting—probably the most important things. And Nikita just made sure the flame burned properly, though from time to time—not too often—he would take a look at Lyuba's face and then stare at the fire again, afraid his look might annoy her. So the time went by, and Nikita thought sorrowfully that soon it would all have gone by and he would have to go home.

At midnight, when the clock chimed from the bell tower, Nikita asked Lyuba why her friend Zhenya had not come.

'She's got typhus again; she's probably going to die,' Lyuba answered—and went back to reading her medicine.

'That's a pity!' said Nikita, but Lyuba did not reply.

Nikita pictured in his mind a sick, feverish Zhenya; no doubt he could sincerely have loved her too if he had known her earlier and if she had been at all kind to him. She too was probably beautiful: it was a shame he couldn't remember her better, that he hadn't been able to make her out more clearly in the dark.

'I want to sleep now,' whispered Lyuba, sighing.

'Have you understood everything you've read?' asked Nikita.

'Perfectly! Do you want to hear it?'

'No. Better keep it to yourself, I'll only forget it.'

He swept up around the stove with a broom and went off to his father's.

From then on he visited Lyuba nearly every day, though sometimes he let a day or two go by so she would miss him. He did not know whether she missed him or not, but on those empty evenings Nikita was compelled to walk ten or fifteen versts, several times round the town, in order to contain his loneliness, to endure his longing for Lyuba and not go to her.

At her house, his usual occupation was keeping the fire going and waiting for Lyuba to say something to him when she looked up from her book. He always brought a little food for Lyuba's supper from the canteen at the furniture workshop; she had a midday meal at the academy, but the portions were too small there, and Lyuba did a lot of thinking and studying, and she was still growing, so she needed more food. The first time he was paid, Nikita bought some

cows' feet in a nearby village and boiled them all night on the iron
stove to make a meat jelly, while Lyuba studied until midnight.

Nikita's father was unhappy being alone in the evening without
his son, and Nikita never told him where he went. 'He's a man in
his own right now,' the old man said to himself. 'He might have been
killed or wounded in the war. But he's alive—so of course he wants
to go out!'

Once the old man noticed that his son had got hold of two white
rolls. But Nikita immediately wrapped them up in a piece of paper
and did not offer his father any. Then he put on his army cap as usual
and was off, probably till midnight, taking both the bread rolls.

'Nikit, take me with you!' his father begged. 'I just want to see
where you go. It must be interesting there, you must be going
somewhere really outstanding!'

'Another time, father,' said Nikita, in embarrassment. 'It's time
you went to bed—tomorrow you've got to work.'

That evening Nikita did not find Lyuba at home. So he sat down
on the bench by the gate and waited for her. He put the white rolls
inside his shirt, to warm them there till Lyuba came back. He sat
there patiently until late into the night, watching the stars in the sky
and the occasional passers-by hurrying home to their children,
listening to the town clock chiming from the bell tower, to dogs
barking in the yards, and to other, less distinct sounds of the night.
He could probably have gone on waiting there until the day he died.

Lyuba appeared soundlessly before Nikita out of the darkness.
He stood up to face her, but she said, 'You'd better go home,' and
burst into tears. She went into the house. Nikita waited a little longer
outside, in bewilderment; then he went in after Lyuba.

'Zhenya has died!' Lyuba told him. 'What shall I do now?'

Nikita said nothing. The warm rolls lay inside his shirt; was it
best to take them out now, or to do nothing at all? Lyuba lay down
fully clothed on her bed, turned her face to the wall and wept silently
with hardly a movement.

Nikita stood a long time in the dark room, ashamed to disturb
someone else's grief. Lyuba paid no attention to him, because sorrow
makes people indifferent to all other sufferers. Nikita sat down on
the bed at Lyuba's feet and took the rolls out from under his shirt,

meaning to put them down somewhere, but unable to find the right place for them.

'Let me stay with you now!' said Nikita.

'But what will you do?' asked Lyuba, in tears.

Nikita thought for a while, afraid of making a mistake or somehow offending her.

'I won't do anything,' he replied. 'We'll live life as usual, so you won't be unhappy.'

'Let's wait, there's no need to hurry,' Lyuba pronounced thoughtfully and prudently. 'We have to think what to bury Zhenya in—they haven't got a coffin.'

'I'll bring one tomorrow,' Nikita promised, and put the rolls down on the bed.

Next day Nikita got permission from the foreman and began making a coffin; they were always free to make coffins and the cost was not docked from their wages. Being unskilled, he took a long time over it, but he was especially careful to give a clean finish to the inside, where the dead girl would be resting. He too was upset at the thought of Zhenya being dead, and he let a few tears drop among the shavings. His father, passing through the yard, went up to Nikita and noticed his distress.

'What are you sad about? Has your girl died?' he asked.

'No, her friend has,' Nikita answered.

'Her friend? Who cares about her! Let me plane off the sides of that coffin for you. You haven't done it right, it looks a mess!'

After work, Nikita took the coffin to Lyuba; he did not know where her dead friend was lying.

There was a long warm autumn that year, and people were glad. 'Harvest was poor but we'll save on firewood,' said thrifty folk. Well in advance, Nikita Firsov had ordered a woman's coat for Lyuba to be made from his Red Army greatcoat; this coat was now ready, though there was no need for it yet because of the warm weather. As before, Nikita visited Lyuba in her home to help her live and, in return, to receive nourishment for the pleasure of his own heart.

Once he asked her how they would live in the future—together or apart? But she answered that it was not possible for her to feel

her happiness until the spring, because she had to finish at the medical academy as fast as she could; then they would see. Nikita heard this distant promise; he was not asking for a greater happiness than that which, thanks to Lyuba, was already his, and he did not know whether a better happiness even existed, but his heart was chilled from long endurance and from uncertainty: did Lyuba really need someone like him—a man who was poor and uneducated and demobilized? Sometimes Lyuba smiled at him with her bright eyes, her face filled with kindness.

Once, as he was covering Lyuba up for the night before going home, Nikita began to weep, but Lyuba just stroked his head and said: 'That's enough of that, you mustn't be so unhappy while I'm still alive.'

Nikita hurried to his father's, to hide away there, recover his spirits, and not go to Lyuba's for several days in a row. 'I'll read,' he resolved, 'and start living properly. I'll forget Lyuba. I won't have anything to do with her. What's so special about her? There are millions and millions of women in the world, some of them even better than she is! She's not that good-looking!'

In the morning he did not get up from his place on the floor. As his father left for work, he felt Nikita's head and said: 'You're hot: lie on the bed! Be ill for a while, then you'll get better. You weren't wounded anywhere in the war, were you?'

'No,' answered Nikita, 'nowhere.'

Towards evening he lost consciousness. At first all he saw was the ceiling, and on it two belated half-dead flies, sheltering there for warmth to prolong their lives; they filled him with melancholy and disgust, but they seemed to have got inside his head and he was unable to drive them out. Nikita shut his eyes, but the flies seethed in his brain; he jumped up from the bed to chase them from the ceiling, and fell back against the pillow; the pillow seemed to smell of his mother's breath—she had slept there beside his father. Nikita remembered her, and forgot himself in unconsciousness.

After four days Lyuba found out where Nikita Firsov lived and came to visit him for the first time. It was the middle of the day, the workers' houses were all empty—the women had gone out to buy provisions, and the children who were not yet at school were roaming

Andrei Platonov

about the yards and open spaces. Lyuba sat on Nikita's bed, stroked his forehead, wiped his eyes with the corner of her handkerchief and asked: 'Now, how do you feel? Are you hurting anywhere?'

'No,' said Nikita, 'nowhere.'

A high fever was carrying him far away from his surroundings, and it was difficult for him to see Lyuba and remember who she was; afraid of losing her in the darkness of his mind, he reached out and grasped the pocket of her coat—the coat that had been sewn from his Red Army greatcoat—and clung on to it like an exhausted swimmer clinging to a sheer rock, half drowning, half saved. The illness was pulling him towards an empty shining horizon, out into the open sea, so he could rest there on its slow heavy waves.

'I'll cure you. You've probably got the flu,' said Lyuba. 'Or maybe it's typhus. But don't worry, it's nothing to be afraid of!'

She pulled Nikita up by his shoulders and sat him with his back to the wall. Quickly and determinedly she dressed him in her coat, found his father's scarf and tied it round the sick man's head, and pushed his feet into some felt boots that were lying under the bed waiting for winter. With her arms around him, she told him to put one foot in front of the other and then led him, shivering, out on to the street. A cab was waiting there. Lyuba seated the sick man inside it and they drove off.

'Seems like none of us are long for this world!' said the driver, addressing the horse and urging it with the reins into a gentle trot.

In her own room Lyuba undressed Nikita, put him in the bed and wrapped him up in a blanket, a strip of old carpet, her mother's decrepit shawl—all the warm things she possessed.

'Why lie there at home?' Lyuba said with satisfaction, tucking the blanket under Nikita's hot body. 'What's the point? Your father's at work, you're alone all day long; there's no one to look after you, and you pine for me.'

For a long time Nikita tried to work out where Lyuba had got the money for the cab. Perhaps she had sold her Austrian shoes or her textbook (she would first have learned it by heart so she didn't need it any more), or else she had paid the cab driver her entire monthly stipend.

Nikita lay there during the night in confused consciousness:

sometimes he knew where he was and could see Lyuba, who was keeping the stove going and cooking food on it, but then he would observe unknown visions of his mind, which was acting independently of his will in the hot, pressured tightness of his head.

His feverish chill kept getting worse. From time to time Lyuba put her palm to his brow and felt the pulse at his wrist. Late in the night she gave him a drink of warm, boiled water; then, taking off her dress, she lay down beside the sick man under the blanket, because Nikita was shivering from the fever and he had to be kept warm. Lyuba embraced Nikita and pressed him to her, while he curled up into a ball against the cold and pressed his face to her breast, to sense close to him someone else's higher, better life and to forget for a while his own torment, his empty body that was chilled right through. Nikita felt it would be a pity to die now—not because he cared about himself, but because he wanted to go on touching Lyuba and another life—so he asked Lyuba in a whisper whether he would get better or die: she had studied and so she must know.

Lyuba hugged Nikita's head in her arms and answered him, 'You'll soon be better. People die because they are ill and have no one to love them, but now you're with me.' Nikita began to feel warm and fell asleep.

Three weeks later, Nikita had recovered. Snow had now fallen outside, everything had gone suddenly quiet, and Nikita went to his father's for the winter. He did not want to disturb Lyuba until she had finished at the academy: let her mind develop to the full, all of it—she too was one of the poor. The father was pleased to see his son again, although he had visited him every third day, always bringing food for his son and some sort of treat for Lyuba.

In the daytime Nikita began working at the workshop again and in the evenings he visited Lyuba, and the winter passed by uneventfully: he knew that in the spring she would be his wife and a long happy life would then begin. Sometimes Lyuba would touch him, push him about, run away from him round the room, and then—after their game—Nikita would cautiously kiss her cheek. But usually Lyuba did not let him touch her affectionately.

'Otherwise you'll get tired of me, and we've still got our whole lives to live!' she said. 'Anyway, I'm not such a tasty morsel. You only think I am!'

On their days off, Lyuba and Nikita went for walks along wintry paths out of town, or else walked a long way downstream, half embracing, along the ice of the sleeping Potudan. Nikita would lie on his stomach and look down through the ice to the quietly flowing water. Lyuba settled down next to him and, their bodies touching, they watched the hidden flow of the water and talked of how lucky the Potudan was, because it went all the way to the sea, and this water under the ice would flow past shores of distant lands where flowers were now growing and birds were singing. After thinking about this for a while, Lyuba would tell Nikita to get up from the ice at once: Nikita now wore his father's old padded jacket, it was too short and not very warm, and he might catch cold.

And so they were friends, patiently, almost all the long winter, tormented by anticipation of their approaching future happiness. The Potudan River also hid under the ice all winter, and the winter crops slumbered beneath the snow. Nikita was calmed and even comforted by these processes of nature: it was not only his heart that lay buried until the spring. In February, when he woke in the morning, he would listen hard to hear whether new flies were buzzing yet; and when he went outside he looked at the sky and at the trees in the next-door garden—to see if the first birds were flying in from faraway places. But the trees, the grasses and the flies were all still asleep in the depth of their strength, in embryo.

In the middle of February Lyuba told Nikita that the final exams would begin on the twentieth, as doctors were greatly needed and the people could not wait for them any longer. And by March the exams would be over: so who cared if the snow lay on the ground and the river flowed under the ice right up to the month of July? Their hearts' happiness would begin before the warmth of nature.

Nikita decided to leave the town until March, to make the time pass quicker before his shared life with Lyuba began. He volunteered to go with a team of joiners from the furniture workshop to repair furniture in village soviets and schools.

Around this time, towards the beginning of March, his father built a large wardrobe as a present for the young people, like the one that had stood in Lyuba's home when her mother had, more or less, been his intended. The old man understood this, how life came full circle as it slipped by, but there was little he could do about it, and with a sigh he put the wardrobe on a sledge and took it to the home of his son's bride-to-be. The snow had grown warmer and was melting in the sun, but the old man was still strong and he dragged the sledge stubbornly on, even over the black body of the bare earth. Secretly he believed that he could perfectly well have married this Lyuba himself, since he had been too shy with her mother, but he felt somehow ashamed and he had nothing at home with which to attract and please a young girl like her. And he concluded that life just wasn't normal. His son was scarcely back from the war, and now he was leaving home again, this time for ever. It was clear that he himself, an old man, would have to take someone in, even if it were only a beggar woman off the street—not so as to have a family life, but so that there would be another living being, like a tame hedgehog or rabbit, about the house: never mind if the creature unsettles your life and spreads dirt everywhere—without it you cease to be human.

As he gave Lyuba the wardrobe, Nikita's father asked her when he would be coming to her wedding. 'As soon as Nikita comes back. I'm ready!' said Lyuba.

That night Nikita's father walked twenty versts to the village where Nikita was at work making school desks. Nikita was asleep on the floor in an empty classroom, but his father woke him and told him it was time to go back to the town: he could get married.

'You go. I'll finish the desks for you,' said the father.

Nikita put on his cap and at once, without waiting for daybreak, set off on foot for the town. All through the second half of the night he walked alone through empty places; the wind from the fields wandered aimlessly around him, now grazing his face, now blowing against his back, and sometimes withdrawing altogether into the ravine beside the path. The earth lay dark on the slopes and on the high ploughland, the snow had run off into the hollows, and there was a smell of young water and of the old grass that had lain there since autumn. But autumn was a long-ago, forgotten time—the earth was now poor and free, it was going to give birth to everything all over again, to creatures that had never lived before. Nikita was not even in a hurry to get to Lyuba; he liked being in the gloomy light of this early earth which had no memory and had forgotten all who had died on it, and which did not know that it would be giving birth in the warmth of a new summer.

Towards morning Nikita arrived at Lyuba's house. A light frost lay on the familiar roof—Lyuba was probably sound asleep now in her warm bed. Nikita walked past the house in order not to wake his bride. He would not make her body cold for the sake of his own comfort.

By the evening Nikita Firsov and Lyuba Kuznetsova had registered their marriage at the district soviet; they then went back to Lyuba's room and did not know what to do. Nikita felt ashamed now that complete happiness had arrived for him—the person he needed most of all in the world wanted to live one life with him, as if some great and precious good lay hidden inside him. He took Lyuba's hand and held it a long time, enjoying the warmth of the palm of this hand; through it he felt the distant beating of a heart that loved him, and he wondered: why did Lyuba love him? For his part, he knew exactly why Lyuba was dear to him.

'First, let's eat!' said Lyuba and took her hand away from Nikita.

She had done some cooking that day: now that she had graduated from the academy, both her stipend and her rations had been increased.

Shyly Nikita started eating the tasty food his wife had prepared. He could not remember ever being given food as a gift, and he had never had occasion to visit people for his own pleasure, still less to eat his fill with them.

After the meal, Lyuba was first to get up from the table. She opened her arms to embrace Nikita and said: 'Well!'

Nikita stood up and timidly embraced her, afraid of harming something in this special, tender body. Lyuba tried to help by clasping him to herself, but Nikita begged, 'Wait, my heart hurts,' and Lyuba let her husband go.

It was growing dark outside, and Nikita made to kindle a fire for some light, but Lyuba said, 'There's no need—I've finished my studies, and today is our wedding day.' Nikita then turned down the bed. At the same time Lyuba undressed in front of him, feeling no shame before her husband. But Nikita went behind the wardrobe his father had made and quickly took his clothes off there, then lay down beside Lyuba for the night.

In the morning Nikita got up early. He swept the room, lit the stove to boil the kettle, went to the entrance for a bucket of water so they could wash, till in the end he could think of nothing more to do while Lyuba slept. He sat down on a chair and hung his head: now Lyuba would probably tell him to go back to his father's, because it turned out that one had to know how to enjoy pleasure. But Nikita could not torment Lyuba for the sake of his own happiness, and all his strength pounded away in his heart, flowing into his throat and lodging there.

Lyuba woke up and watched her husband.

'Don't be downhearted, it's not worth it,' she said with a smile. 'Everything will work out all right.'

'Let me scrub the floor,' Nikita begged. 'It doesn't look clean.'

'All right,' she agreed.

'He's so sad and weak—and all because he loves me!' Lyuba thought, in bed. 'How I love him, how precious he is to me. So what if I stay a virgin for ever! I can endure that. Or maybe one day he'll love me less, and that'll make him strong.' Nikita was working at the floor with a wet rag, scrubbing the dirt from the boards, and Lyuba laughed at him as she lay in the bed.

'So here I am, a married woman,' she thought joyfully, slipping out from under the blanket in her nightdress.

After tidying the room, Nikita wiped all the furniture with a damp cloth, then added hot water to the cold water in the pail and pulled out a basin from under the bed for Lyuba to wash in.

Lyuba drank her tea, kissed her husband on the forehead and went off to her work at the hospital, saying she would be back about three o'clock. Nikita put his hand to the place on his forehead where his wife had kissed him, and remained alone. He was not sure why he had not gone to work that day; it felt shameful to go on living now, and perhaps it would be better if he did not—what reason, then, was there for him to earn his daily bread? But he made up his mind somehow to live his life through, until he wasted away from shame and misery.

After taking stock of their family possessions, Nikita found some food and prepared a single dish for their meal—millet gruel with some meat. But after this work he lay face down on the bed and began calculating how much time was left before the rivers started to flow again and he could drown himself in the Potudan.

'I'll wait till the ice shifts: it won't be long!' he said out loud to calm himself, and dozed off.

Lyuba brought two pots of winter flowers home from work—a wedding present from the doctors and nurses there. She had behaved importantly and mysteriously with them, like a real woman. The young girls among the sisters and nurses had envied her and one candid woman in the hospital pharmacy had trustingly asked Lyuba whether or not it was true that love was something magical, and that marrying for love was an intoxicating happiness. Lyuba had answered that this was perfectly true—which was why people lived in the world.

In the evening husband and wife had a talk. Lyuba said they must think about the children they might have. Nikita promised to start making children's furniture at the workshop after hours: a little table, a chair and a rocking cradle.

'The Revolution's here to stay, now's a good time to bear children,' said Nikita. 'Children will never be unhappy again.'

'It's all right for you to talk, but it's me who'll be giving birth to them,' said Lyuba, piqued.

'Will it hurt?' asked Nikita. 'Don't have any, then. Why make yourself suffer?'

'Oh, I dare say I'll manage!' said Lyuba.

At dusk she made up the bed and, so there would be more room, she brought up two chairs for their feet and said the two of them should lie across the bed. Nikita lay down where she told him to, fell silent, and late in the night began crying in his sleep. Lyuba, though, could not sleep for a long time; she heard Nikita crying and carefully wiped his sleeping face with the edge of the sheet—and when he woke up in the morning he did not remember his night-time sorrow.

From then on their life together went along at its own pace. Lyuba tended people at the hospital, and Nikita made peasant furniture. In his spare time and on Sundays he worked in the house and about the yard, although Lyuba never asked him to. She was no longer quite sure whose house it was. First, it had belonged to her mother, then it had been taken over by the State, but the State had forgotten about it—nobody ever came to collect any rent or to check that the house was intact. None of this mattered to Nikita. He got hold of some green paint through friends of his father's and he gave a fresh coat to the roof and shutters as soon as the spring weather had settled in. With the same diligence he gradually repaired the ramshackle shed outside, mended the gates and the fence and prepared to dig a new cellar, since the old one had fallen in.

The River Potudan had begun to stir. Twice Nikita went to its bank, looked at the now-flowing water and decided not to die so long as Lyuba could still put up with him; when she stopped putting up with him, he would have time enough to end his life—it would be a while yet before the river froze again. Nikita usually worked slowly on his outside jobs, so as not to sit in the room and vex Lyuba to no purpose. And when he had done everything there was to do, he would scrape up some clay from the old cellar into the flap of his shirt and carry it into their room. He would then sit on the floor and fashion the clay into small human figures and a variety of objects that had no function or likeness to anything—a mountain with an animal head growing out of it, or a huge tree-root so intricate and impenetrable, with each branch biting into the next, gnawing itself and tormenting itself, that looking at this root for any length of time made you want to sleep. As he worked at the clay Nikita smiled, unthinkingly and blissfully, and Lyuba sat there beside him on the floor mending clothes, singing little songs she had once heard, and in between her work she would caress Nikita with one hand, stroking his head or tickling him under the arm. Nikita lived through these hours with clenched and gentle heart, and did not know whether he still needed something mightier and more elevated, or whether life really was nothing so very great, nothing more than he already had. But Lyuba looked at him with tired eyes that were full of patient kindness, as though goodness and happiness had become a heavy labour for her. Then Nikita would crush his toys, turning them back into clay, and ask his wife if he should stoke up the stove to heat some water for tea, or if there was any errand he should do for her.

'No, no,' Lyuba would smile. 'I can do everything myself.'

And Nikita would realize that life was indeed something great and perhaps beyond his strength, that not all of it was concentrated in his beating heart. It was more interesting still, more powerful, more precious, in another human being whom he could not reach. He took the bucket and went off to the town well, where the water was cleaner than in the tanks on the street. There was nothing, no task, that could wear out his grief and Nikita was afraid, just as in his childhood, of the approaching night. After drawing the water, he called in on his father, carrying the full bucket, and sat in his house for a while.

'Why didn't you have a proper wedding?' asked the father. 'You got married on the quiet—soviet fashion, didn't you?'

'We'll have a wedding yet,' his son promised. 'Let's make a small table together, and a chair and a cradle. You talk to the foreman tomorrow and get the materials. After all, we'll probably be having children.'

'All right, I can do that,' the father agreed. 'But you won't be having children that soon. It's early days.'

Within a week Nikita had made all the children's furniture they needed; he had stayed on late every evening and worked diligently. And his father had given each piece a clean finish and painted it.

Lyuba arranged the furniture in a special corner, adorned the future child's little table with the two pots of flowers, and hung a new embroidered towel over the back of the chair. In gratitude for his loyalty to her and to her unknown children Lyuba hugged Nikita, kissed him on the throat, pressed him against her chest and warmed herself for a long time beside this loving man, knowing this was all she could do. And Nikita, with his arms hanging down, hiding his heart, stood silently before her, not wanting to appear strong when he was helpless.

That night Nikita was unable to sleep for long, and he woke soon after midnight. He lay a long while in the silence and listened to the sound of the town clock—half past twelve, one o'clock, half past one. In the sky outside the window a vague stirring had begun; it was not yet dawn, only a movement of the darkness, a slow baring of empty space, and all the things in the room and the new children's furniture became visible, though they appeared pitiful and exhausted after the dark night they had lived through, as if pleading for help. Lyuba shifted under the blanket and sighed: perhaps she too was not asleep. Just in case, Nikita kept still and listened. But Lyuba did not move again, she was breathing evenly, and Nikita felt pleased that she was lying beside him, alive, necessary to his soul and not remembering in her sleep that he, her husband, existed. As long as she was whole, and happy! As for himself, the mere consciousness of Lyuba was enough to keep him alive. And Nikita dozed off in peace, drawing comfort from the sleep of this close and loved being. Then he opened his eyes again.

Carefully, almost inaudibly, Lyuba was crying. She had pulled the blanket over her head and was alone there in her distress, choking back her grief so it would die soundlessly. Nikita turned his face towards Lyuba: she had curled up pathetically under the blanket and was breathing fast, in anguish. Nikita did not speak. Not every grief can be comforted; there is a grief which ends only after the heart has been worn away in long oblivion, or in distraction amid life's everyday concerns.

At dawn Lyuba quietened down. Nikita let some time pass, then lifted the top of the blanket and looked at his wife's face. She was sleeping peacefully, warm and still, her tears now dried.

Nikita rose, dressed himself without a sound and went outside. A feeble morning was beginning in the world. A beggar was walking down the middle of the street with a full bag and Nikita set out after this man, just for the purpose of going somewhere. The beggar walked on out of the town and set off along the high road to the settlement of Kantemirovka where there had always been big markets and a prosperous population: true, they never gave much to beggars there—if you wanted food you had to go to the poorer villages further off; nonetheless Kantemirovka was lively and interesting and at the market you could live just by watching the throngs of people, as they took your mind off things for a time.

The beggar and Nikita arrived in Kantemirovka towards noon. On the outskirts of the town the beggar man sat down in a shallow ditch, opened his bag and began to feed himself and Nikita from it; but in the town they went their different ways, as the beggar had plans of his own, and Nikita had none. Nikita reached the market, sat down in the shade behind a stall and ceased thinking about Lyuba, about life's cares and about himself.

The market watchman had been living at the market for twenty-five years, and all that time he and his stout, childless wife had eaten lavishly. The traders and the people at the cooperative stores had always given him their butcher's waste and bits of reject meat, and they let him have cloth at cost price, as well as such household necessities as thread and soap. For some time now he had been trading in a small way himself, selling off damaged empty crates and hoarding money at the savings bank. His duties were to sweep the whole market clean of rubbish, to wash the blood from the butchers' slabs, to clean the public latrines, and to keep watch at night over the stalls and storage places. But the hard work was done by the vagabonds and beggars who spent the night there, and he did nothing himself except stroll around at night in a warm sheepskin coat; his wife usually poured out the remains of yesterday's cabbage and meat soup into a slop pail, so the watchman could always get some poor fellow to clean the latrines in return for food.

His wife was forever telling him not to do the hard work, for just look how grey his beard had grown—he was a supervisor now, not a watchman.

But you cannot get a tramp or a beggar to perform eternal labour in return for food: he will do the work once, eat what he is given, ask for more, then disappear back into the countryside.

Recently, several nights in a row, the watchman had driven the same man out of the market. When the watchman gave him a push as he slept, the man would get up and move on without answering back—and then there he was again, lying behind a distant stall. Once the watchman chased this homeless man all night long, his blood leaping from the desire to torment and vanquish an alien and exhausted being. A couple of times the watchman threw a stick at him and hit him on the head, but at dawn the vagabond gave him the slip—he seemed to have left the market place altogether. Then in the morning the watchman found him again; he was asleep on the roof of the cesspit, behind the latrines. The watchman called to the sleeping man, who opened his eyes but said nothing; he just looked at him and dozed off again indifferently. The watchman decided the man was dumb. He poked the point of a stick into the sleeper's stomach and gestured to him to follow.

The watchman took the man to the neat apartment—one room and a separate kitchen—that went with his job. There the watchman offered him a little cold cabbage soup, with pork-rind, straight from the pot, and then told him to take a broom, a spade, a scraper and a bucket of lime from the entrance and go and clean up the public latrines. The dumb man looked at the watchman with vague eyes: probably he was deaf too... But no, not at all. The dumb man went to the entrance and took all the tools and materials he needed, just as the watchman had instructed him.

Nikita did the work efficiently, and later the watchman came out to check how he had got on. It was not a bad start, so the watchman took Nikita to where the horses were tethered, and entrusted him with the job of collecting the dung and taking it out on a wheelbarrow.

At home the watchman instructed his wife to stop throwing the remains of lunch and supper into the slop pail, and to pour them instead into a separate bowl: let the dumb man finish them up.

'Soon you'll be telling me to make up a bed for him in our room!' said the mistress of the house.

'Nonsense!' stated the watchman. 'He's going to sleep outside. He isn't deaf, you know, so let him lie there and listen out for thieves. If he hears anything, he can come and get me. Give him some sacking—he can find himself somewhere to sleep.'

Nikita lived a long time at the town market. Having lost the habit of speaking, he then began to think less, to remember less and suffer less. Only now and then did a weight settle on his heart, but he bore it without reflection, and gradually the feeling of grief inside him wore itself out and went away. He had grown used to living at the market; the crowds, the hum of the voices, and the daily goings-on distracted him from his memory and his own needs—food, rest, and the desire to see his father. Nikita worked constantly: even at night when he was falling asleep in an empty crate in the middle of the silent market place, the supervisor-watchman would come over and tell him to doze lightly, to keep listening and not sleep the sleep of the dead. 'Anything can happen,' the watchman would say. 'The other day robbers tore two boards off a stall and ate a whole *pood* of honey without any bread...' By dawn Nikita was already at work, hurrying to clean up the market before the crowds came; during the day there was not even time to eat—there was dung to be shovelled from a heap on to the communal cart, or a new pit to be dug for slops and filth, or else he had to break up the old crates which the watchman got for nothing from the traders and then sold as planks to people from the village.

In the middle of the summer Nikita was put in prison on suspicion of stealing chandler's goods from the market branch of the agricultural cooperative, but the investigation cleared him—this dumb and worn-out man was too indifferent to the charge against him. The investigator could not find in Nikita's character, or in the humble work he did at the market as watchman's assistant, any sign of greed for life or desire for pleasure or enjoyment—even in prison he did not eat all his food. The investigator realized that this man did not know the value of either personal or public property, nor was there any clear evidence in the circumstances of the case. 'Not worth dirtying a prison with a man like him!' the investigator decided.

Nikita spent only five days in prison, and then went straight back to the market. The watchman-supervisor was exhausted from doing the work on his own, so he was glad when the dumb man showed up again. The old man asked Nikita into his apartment and gave him some freshly made hot soup, thus infringing his household regime of thriftiness. 'Just one meal—it won't ruin us!' the old watchman-boss reassured himself. 'Then it'll be back to yesterday's cold leftovers—when there are any!'

'Go and rake up the rubbish from the grocery stalls,' the watchman ordered, when Nikita had finished eating the soup.

Nikita went off to his usual work. By now his sense of his own self was weak and he thought only those thoughts which wandered into his mind at random. By autumn, most likely, he would have quite forgotten what he was, and, when he saw the world going on around him, would no longer have any idea what it meant; he might seem to everyone else to be living his life in the world, but in fact he would just happen to be there, existing in unconsciousness, in poverty of mind, in absence of feeling, as if in some homely warmth, hiding from mortal grief.

Not long after he had been in prison, when summer was coming to an end and the nights were lengthening, Nikita was about to lock the door to the latrines—as was required by the rules—when he heard a voice from inside. 'You there, wait a minute, don't lock up yet! There's nothing worth stealing in here, is there?'

Nikita waited for the person to leave. Out of the latrine came his father, with an empty sack under his arm.

'Hello, Nikit,' said his father—and suddenly began to weep pitifully, ashamed of his tears and not wiping them away, refusing to acknowledge their existence. 'We thought you were dead and gone long ago. So you're all right?'

Nikita embraced his thin, bowed father, and his heart, that had grown unused to feeling, began to stir.

They went into the empty market place and sheltered in the passage between two stalls.

'I came here for buckwheat, it's cheaper here,' his father explained. 'But I was late, see, the market's already packed up. So I'll spend the night here, buy some tomorrow, then go back. But what are you doing here?'

Nikita wanted to reply to his father, but his throat had dried up and he had forgotten how to speak. He had a fit of coughing and then managed to whisper, 'I'm all right. Is Lyuba alive?'

'She threw herself in the river,' said the father. 'But some fishermen saw her straight away. They pulled her out and brought her round. She was even in hospital. She got better.'

'And she's alive now?' asked Nikita quietly.

'Well, she hasn't died yet,' said the father. 'Blood often comes from her throat: she must have caught a chill when she was drowning. She chose a bad time—the weather had turned nasty, the water was cold.'

The father took some bread from his pocket and gave half to his son and they ate a little of it for their supper. Nikita was silent, and his father spread his sack on the ground, getting ready to settle down for the night.

'Have you got a place yourself?' asked the father. 'If not, you lie on the sack and I'll lie on the ground. I won't catch cold, I'm old.'

'Why did Lyuba drown herself?' whispered Nikita.

'You got a sore throat or something?' asked his father. 'That'll pass. She was unhappy, she was wasting away with grief for you—that's why. For a whole month she walked up and down the bank of the Potudan, she'd walk a hundred versts each way. She thought you'd drowned and would float to the top, and she wanted to see you. And it turns out you were here all the time. That's bad…'

Nikita thought of Lyuba, and his heart once more began to fill with grief and strength.

'Sleep here on your own, father,' said Nikita, 'I'll go and have a look at Lyuba.'

'You get going,' his father agreed. 'It's a good time for walking, it's cool. I'll be along tomorrow, we'll talk then.'

Nikita left the town and began running along the deserted highroad. When he felt exhausted, he dropped to a walking pace for a while, and then ran again in the weightless air over the dark fields.

Late at night Nikita knocked at Lyuba's window and touched the shutters he had once painted with green paint—in the dark night they looked blue. He pressed his face to the window pane. A faint light spread through the room from a white sheet that was hanging off the bed, and Nikita could see the children's furniture he and his father had made—it was all still there. Then Nikita knocked loudly on the window frame. But again Lyuba did not answer, she did not come up to the window to see that it was him.

Nikita climbed over the gate, went into the entrance, then into the room. The doors were not locked: whoever lived here did not bother to protect their property from thieves.

Lyuba was lying on the bed, even her head hidden beneath the blanket.

'Lyuba!' Nikita called softly.

'What?' asked Lyuba from under the blanket.

She was not asleep. Perhaps she felt ill and afraid as she lay there on her own, or perhaps she thought that the knock at the window and Nikita's voice were a dream.

Nikita sat down on the edge of the bed.

'Lyuba, it's me, I've come.'

Lyuba threw the blanket off her face. 'Come to me quickly,' she begged in her old tender voice, and held her arms out to Nikita.

Lyuba was afraid all this would suddenly vanish; she seized Nikita by the arms and pulled him to her.

Nikita embraced Lyuba with the force that tries to take the other, the beloved, inside one's yearning soul; but he quickly remembered himself and felt ashamed.

'Not hurting, are you?' asked Nikita.

'No! I'm not,' answered Lyuba.

He wanted her, all of her, so she would be comforted, and a cruel, pitiful strength came to him. But Nikita's joy from this close love of Lyuba was nothing higher than what he had known ordinarily; he felt only that his heart was now in command of all his body, sharing its blood with a poor but necessary pleasure.

Lyuba asked Nikita if he would light the stove—it would be dark outside for a long time yet. A fire would light up the room, and in any case she didn't want to sleep any more, she would wait for dawn and look at Nikita.

But there was no more firewood in the entrance. So Nikita ripped two boards off the shed in the yard, chopped them into kindling and lit the iron stove. When the fire had got going, Nikita opened the little door to let the light out. Lyuba got down from the bed and sat on the floor where it was light, facing Nikita.

'Will it be all right now, you won't mind living with me?' she asked.

'It'll be all right,' answered Nikita. 'I've got used to being happy with you now.'

'Put more wood on the fire, I'm freezing,' said Lyuba.

She was wearing only a threadbare nightdress, and her thin body was chilled to the bone in the cool half-dark of the late time.   □

GROWN UP ALL WRONG
75 Great Rock and Pop Artists from Vaudeville to Techno

ROBERT CHRISTGAU

Robert Christgau's writings, collected here, are an encyclopedia of popular music over the past fifty years, ranging from the 1950s singer-songwriter tradition through hip-hop, alternative, and beyond. With unfailing style, Christgau negotiates the straits of great music, thorny politics, and commerce. He illuminates legends from pop music and the beginnings of rock and roll—George Gershwin, Nat King Cole, and Elvis Presley—and looks at the subtle transition to plain "rock" in the music of Janis Joplin, the Rolling Stones, James Brown, and others. This is the music of the second half of the twentieth century, skillfully framed by a writer whose reach, insight, and perfect pitch make him one of the major cultural critics of our time.

New in cloth

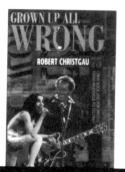

PLACE FOR US
Essay on the Broadway Musical

D.A. MILLER

"[This book] anatomizes a sentimental and cliché-ridden mass-cultural form that Miller frankly admits no politically savvy individual would willingly embrace. Instead, he argues, the classic Broadway musical chooses its audience, selecting, as a tigress does the slowest antelope in the herd, gay men as the easiest prey... Miller has a knack for making good points with good jokes...But Miller's humor here shouldn't surprise us. Given the compromises required of a professor writing about such an abasing medium as Broadway, he carries the show with a bravura worthy of Merman herself. And like La Merm, he compels us at the same time to take his song and dance in earnest."
—Michael Trask,
LINGUA FRANCA
New in cloth

IN SEARCH OF AFRICA

MANTHIA DIAWARA

In 1996 Manthia Diawara, a distinguished professor of film and literature in New York City, returned to Guinea, thirty-two years after he and his family were expelled from the newly liberated country. The Africa he found was neither the one on the verge of barbarism, as described in the Western press, nor the Africa of his childhood, when the excitement of independence made everything seem possible for young Africans. This book gives us the story of a quest for a childhood friend, for the past and present, and above all for an Africa that is struggling to find its future.

"[This] is one of the most outstanding works of cultural criticism/memoir I have ever read. It is dazzling in its range and extraordinarily compassionate in its judgments."
—Houston A. Baker, Jr.
New in cloth

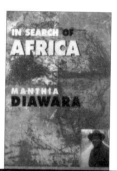

HARVARD UNIVERSITY PRESS
US: 800 448 2242 • UK: 0171 306 0603 • www.hup.harvard.edu

GRANTA

MY GRANDMOTHER, THE CENSOR

Masha Gessen

Ester (left) and Rozalia in the Crimea, 1950s

'Hungarian! Who invented it? My brain couldn't retain a single word—not "thank you", not "hello", not "one", "two" or "three". I've never felt so much like a foreigner.'

I am complaining. I have just come to Moscow after reporting a story in the Balkans. It is 1993. I am an American journalist, but for the previous couple of years I have been spending more and more time in Moscow, the city of my birth. I am getting to know my two grandmothers, who were left behind when my family left for the United States in 1981, when I was fourteen.

'Ah, Hungarian,' says my grandmother as we step off the bus into the sleeting greyness of a Moscow spring. 'Never could wrap my mind around it either. Italian, Czech, Romanian, Polish—none of those were a problem. German, French and English, of course, I knew. But Hungarian—no matter how much I struggled, I could not get past the dictionary.'

I stare down at my grandmother in surprise. I know she translates books from English and German, and that she also knows French. But Czech, Romanian, Polish? 'What's with all the languages?' I ask. 'I never knew you translated from those.'

Or did I? Let me recall what I knew before we stepped off the bus.

I knew that my grandmother Rozalia, Baba Ruzya to me, was a member of the Communist Party. When I was about ten and torn between the nauseating (but appealing) aesthetic fed to me at school and the compelling dissident sympathies of my parents, my mother told me that Baba Ruzya belonged to the Party. Reared in a closed circle of Jewish intellectual types I was not aware of anyone else I knew being a member.

'Baba,' I asked one day, 'why did you join the Party?'

'Because I believed in the goals and ideals of the Party,' my grandmother said slowly and carefully.

I didn't pay much attention to the past tense or the care in her reply and walked away feeling frustrated with an answer that sounded as if it came out of a school book. What I really wanted to know had nothing to do with this story. I wanted to know why the day I got my red Young Pioneer kerchief was the happiest day of my life. Why, if I had already been reading Solzhenitsyn? But that was a question about belonging, and my grandmothers' stories are about anything but that.

I also knew something else. Sometime in the late 1970s my mother got her hands on a copy of George Orwell's *Nineteen Eighty-four*. She quoted it endlessly; she told stories from it as though they were real-life anecdotes. At the kitchen table one day, she talked, with a high-pitched laugh, about the Ministry of Truth—imagine that! Imagine a place where news is routinely rewritten to fit the ideological line!

'And what do you think I did at Glavlit?' Baba Ruzya asked, slowly and carefully again.

Glavlit. *Glav*, as in *glavny*, or head, the chief. *Lit*, as in *literature*. Meaning the Head Directorate of Literature. Baba Ruzya tells me what she did there as we walk from the bus. At first, for three years, she worked in a department known as the Department of Control over Foreign Media. The control was exercised as soon as the foreign media—books, magazines, anything in print—crossed the border. The post office forwarded all such parcels to Glavlit, where an army of readers, known then as 'political editors', but, later, in their retirement documents, simply called 'censors', examined printed matter for signs of anti-Soviet prejudice.

'Sometimes we stamped them "permitted", and then they were allowed into libraries or shops,' my grandmother says. 'But this hardly ever happened. For the most part, we stamped things "for internal use". I mean, sometimes you could rip a few pages out and clear it, but mostly you just had to ban it. Because there was hardly a magazine or a book where the Soviet Union was not somehow maligned. It's not like people were sending Shakespeare and Dickens across the border. They were sending contemporary literature. All it had to contain was a phrase like, "even such an undemocratic society as the Soviet Union…"—and it would be condemned to a classified library.'

There was one man in Paris who kept sending large quantities of books and magazines to another man in some tiny village in the far north of Russia. Soon after she came to work there, one of the more experienced staff explained that the man in the far north was a member of the pre-revolutionary nobility, a scholar, perhaps a biologist, who had long ago decided not to emigrate. His brother, an artist, had moved to Paris. The scholar was arrested and exiled to the far north. On learning of his brother's fate, the artist decided to try to improve the quality of his life by sending him reading materials. Most of these ended up in classified libraries in Moscow. 'This biologist got tiny crumbs out of those parcels.' Neither, of course, would ever know that more was sent or that less was received: no one was meant to know about the existence of the Department of Control over Foreign Media.

Why was my Baba Ruzya working at Glavlit? She had wanted to be a history teacher. She attended a remarkable school in the centre of Moscow, the enclave of the educated if not always the privileged. They adored their teachers there. But one was especially inspirational. She punctuated her history course with a particular expression: 'And this is no mere coincidence.' Ruzya saw a career in which she could also tell her pupils: 'And this is no mere coincidence.'

'The first, the biggest, mistake I ever made was attending the history department at the university. I knew I could never teach school. I couldn't lie to the children.' And there was another thing. Teachers got paid very little, and Ruzya needed money.

By 1943 she was a twenty-three-year-old war widow with a one-year-old daughter. She had a bed in one of the two rooms that belonged to her parents-in-law in a communal flat in Moscow. She had no milk; it vanished on the day she got the news that her husband had been killed. But she had a friend who said she could get her a job.

The problem with that job was Ruzya's father. 'He was a man who was honest beyond reproach. He never tried to convince me to quit; he just expressed his surprise tenderly.' When he first found out about Glavlit, he said, 'But you are doing a policeman's work.' Otherwise, it was better than school: 'Here I was lying only to myself. As a teacher, I would have had to lie to forty children. Here I lied with a clear conscience, so to speak, because if I hadn't been doing that job, someone else would have. But to lie while looking children in the eye—that would have been terrible.'

In 1946 she had been working at Glavlit for three years. She had passed the annual exams, and she was known to have an aptitude for languages. So when the Soviet government, in a fit of post-war politesse, divorced censorship from diplomacy—transferring the responsibility for censoring foreign correspondents from the Ministry of Foreign Affairs to Glavlit—my grandmother was chosen to work in the new department. It comprised three people who came from Foreign Affairs, three people from the Ministry of State Security (which would later become part of the KGB), and my grandmother.

There were advantages. Unlike the department that controlled foreign media—words coming into the Soviet Union—the department that controlled foreign journalists—words going out—did not lead a secret existence. Its staff had a separate entrance at the Central Telegraph office, where they worked, but that was to prevent the censors from meeting the people they were censoring. The foreign journalists knew they were there: the conditions of accreditation for foreign correspondents were that all dispatches be filed from the Central Telegraph building, where they would be cleared by the censor.

I have loved the Central Telegraph building since I was a child—for its rotating multicoloured globe, its digital clock, and its catholic architectural aspirations. My grandmother's office had a door through which the clerk brought the dispatches, an electric bell she rang when she was done with a piece, and two telephones. She used one for routine calls, and the other when in doubt, to telephone her translation of a text directly to Stalin's secretariat.

Every time a correspondent from a new country was accredited, she was crash-taught his language. German, French and English she knew already. Italian, Czech, Romanian, Polish—none of these were a problem. But Hungarian—no matter how much she struggled, she could not get past the dictionary.

There are two things I ought to make clear. First, almost as soon as she starts telling me about her career (as we wade through the sleet from the bus stop to the market), my grandmother declares that the head of the department, Alexei Lukich Zorin, was a good, decent man.

Second, as I listen to the story, as we wade through the sleet from the bus stop to the market place, I am surprised but not horrified, even though my Baba Ruzya has told me that for eleven key post-war years she censored what the rest of the world could learn about the Soviet Union.

There are certain things she remembers very well. Certain journalists. Walter Cronkite from UPI—he filed a lot of stories, but it was your regular wire copy stuff, dry and dull, 'amazingly boring'. But Max Frankel from the *New York Times*. There was a writer to be savoured. 'He had his own point of view, you see, and he just expressed it how he wanted, so bravely.' She translated his articles in their entirety and sent them by messenger to Stalin's secretary. Hours later, Frankel's 'corrected' copy would go over the wire to New York. Every day at the end of her shift—generally it ended in the morning, since most dispatches went out overnight—she prepared a summary of the day's news for Stalin's office, mainly a circular exercise of translating back into Russian what foreign correspondents had culled from Soviet newspapers—a re-spinning of Soviet stories was pretty much all that was allowed out. 'Altogether I worked at Glavlit for fifteen years, and never in that time did I make a mistake in translation.' I believe her. And anyway, she would have known if she had. Mistakes were lethal.

Certain episodes she remembers very well. The Doctors' Plot episode. The Stalin death episode. The Fellini episode.

The Doctors' Plot began in 1952. She heard of it originally from a typist in the office. But first you have to know how frightened Ruzya was by then of losing her job. The Anti-Cosmopolitan Campaign was entering its fifth year, the fifth year of rabid official anti-Semitism, the fifth year that Jews could not find work or hold on to university places. Without her job, Ruzya and her child would have faced a desperate life. And you have to know that she was the only Jew in the department that controlled foreign correspondents, and that she was the only staff member who did not belong to the Party. By this time she was so afraid of losing her job that she would have joined—but she no longer could, because she was Jewish. And the typist said: 'You know, they are going to exile the Jews to Siberia.'

And then the correspondents began to write stories saying the same thing. It was obvious, really; Stalin had exiled other ethnic groups in their entirety: he had moved the Chechens and the Ingush from the Caucasus to Siberian Kazakhstan; he had moved the Tartars from the Crimea, and the Germans from the Volga; and now that the Jews were the scapegoats of the nation, he would surely move them too. The Anti-Cosmopolitan drama was clearly drawing to a climax, with every Soviet newspaper hot on the heels of the Doctors' Plot, the chilling story of a conspiracy by Jewish doctors to kill innocent Soviet citizens. They were called the 'killers in white coats'. As the story went, there would be show trials, executions in Red Square, and pogroms throughout the country. Then, in a show of saving the Jews, the magnanimous Soviet government would exile them to northern Siberia.

The correspondents kept writing about this likely sequence of events, and she kept crossing it out. It was obvious to her that the stories were true, and it was obvious that she could not let them through, because every day that she did her job well enough to keep it was another day when she might not be deported. In effect, these correspondents were writing for her, reminding her of her future several times every night.

In the day, when she slept, she had a recurring nightmare. She is in a cattle car, cradling her ten-year-old daughter, who is asking for a drink of water. But she has no water.

When important events happened on one of Ruzya's nights off, a messenger would appear at the door. In 1953, she was living with her parents again. In the early hours of 4 March that year, the messenger said, 'Comrade Stalin has died, and Comrade Solodovnik is summoned to work.' Her mother started wailing. Ruzya thought: 'I have a moron for a mother.'

That is how my grandmother remembers it. My own mother had a different memory. She woke up to see her mother dressing for work at four in the morning. 'Mama, what happened?' she said.

'Nothing important, dear. Stalin died. Go back to sleep.'

Here is an episode they both remembered. There would be no classes, the teacher announced on 4 March, because Comrade Stalin had died. The other children wailed. My mother drew a thick black frame, signifying death, around Stalin's portrait in her textbook, and wrote HOLIDAY, signifying no school. Happening to glance at the page, the teacher ripped the textbook out of the girl's hands and summoned her mother to the school.

'Buy your child a new textbook and explain some things to her,' the teacher said. We were lucky to have happened upon a teacher like that, family legend concludes: a teacher who concealed instead of informing.

After Stalin died, there were the days of carnage and fear. Gorky Street, the avenue that led past the Central Telegraph to Red Square, was closed to all vehicles and people. Parallel streets teemed with human traffic, hundreds of thousands who had walked for days to view the body of the Father of the Nation. Those who worked or lived on Gorky Street were issued special passes that enabled them to pass through the barricades of military trucks. My grandmother was one of those let through. 'On my way to work I stopped by the stores, and it was delightful. I was able to buy things I could never have had. I bought calf tongue—imagine, calf tongue!—it cost pennies back then, it's just that you could never get it, but there I was practically the only customer.' But it was frightening. It was still cold, and the truck drivers kept gunning their engines, and the roar of the crowds on the other streets mixed with the roar of the engines and filled the empty street with dread.

She and her child shared a room in a giant communal flat in a basement off Trubnaya Ploshad, a square at the bottom of two hills, just below the streets that led to the Body. People fell over and got trampled in the crush. Bodies rolled down the streets on to Trubnaya Ploshad. They were carried past their basement windows—endlessly, it seemed.

'People said, "He lived in blood and died in blood." But you know, others, the idiots, they cried and cried. It was frightening. And then the happy day came when the newspapers announced that the doctors had been released and the investigation was stopped.' That was on 4 April 1953, a month after Stalin died.

The censors were not allowed to have any contact with the foreign correspondents, though they had all seen my grandmother many

times. As the only young woman in the department—pretty at that—
she was the one designated to attend all the press conferences, posing
as a Soviet correspondent.

A couple of years after Stalin's death, the clerk came in with a
dispatch and a small envelope: 'The Italian correspondents sent this
for you.' The envelope contained a ticket to the morning show of
the Italian film festival. 'It was the first foreign film festival, you
understand? It wasn't international, it was Italian, but it was the first
Western film festival here in the USSR. I was dying to go, but there
was no way to get tickets. The cinemas were swamped. You see, we
had no televisions in the Soviet Union then, no refrigerators even—
these came much later—we had never seen… And there was a ticket,
just a ticket with a seat number, for the morning show right after I
finished work, and there was no note. It was my signal to act.'

She risked her job for a film. Of course, after Stalin's death, she
was risking only her job and nothing else, and after twelve years
she was willing to give it up for a movie. She took precautions. She
arrived at the theatre at the last minute, walked into the hall when
the lights had already dimmed, and slipped out in the dark just before
the end credits came up. 'I never looked to either side of me, I was
so frightened. But of course they saw me.'

She can still recount Fellini's *La Strada* in detail. She has seen it
twice since and cried every time. She says it's a great film.

The correspondents were endlessly fascinated with the censor's
identity (for some reason they all seemed to assume that a single
person read all their dispatches). They even had bets. At one point
they decided the censor was a large man: *he* made heavy pencil marks.

Researching a piece in 1997 on the fortieth anniversary of the
International Youth and Students Conference in Moscow, I discover
that Daniel Schorr, the patriarch of American radio commentary,
served as CBS correspondent in Moscow in 1956–1957.

'You are probably too young to know this,' Schorr tells me on
the telephone, 'but back then in the Soviet Union they had censorship
for foreign correspondents.'

I know, I say. I'm not too young and I'm the censor's
granddaughter. I tell him that she is a woman, a nice old Jewish lady.

I even suggest they could meet should he come to Moscow. He asks me to meet him for lunch.

One of the advantages of personal journalism is that it allows one to say what one *would* have said when one was really at a loss for words. When we meet in a Washington, DC, restaurant about a week later, Daniel Schorr shows me the script of his commentary for National Public Radio. It compares the conversation with me to 'meeting your masked executioner'. In it I suggest that he meets my grandmother but he replies that he could not face a nice little old lady after hating the big guy for forty years. 'Tell her hello,' he says, 'and tell her the rest of the message is deleted.'

I am a little nervous passing the message to my grandmother, but she laughs. You should hear Baba Ruzya laugh, the way it rings and rolls like the Russian 'r'.

'I've already called some of the guys and told them,' Daniel Schorr tells me at lunch. 'I hope you don't mind.' He is eighty-seven.

Almost a year later, one of the 'guys' calls. Martin Calb, head of the media centre at Harvard, is going to Moscow, where he served in 1959, and he wants to meet my grandmother. I'm sorry, I say, she didn't censor you, she was already gone. He wants to meet her anyway.

She is nervous about meeting him. Will he want to know secrets? That's not right: she did promise not to tell. Will he want to know about her? Why would he?

She just talks and tells her stories until Calb and his wife have to interrupt her because a bus is taking them to a Kremlin reception. She tells me to finish telling him the story sometime, to tell him about how she left Glavlit. 'He is so handsome,' she smiles.

Weeks later, I get a letter from Calb thanking me for the meeting and suggesting I apply for a fellowship at his centre. The idea that my grandmother's job as a censor could get me a fellowship at Harvard strikes me as funny, but I don't write back because I'm disorganized and basically lazy.

The story of how she left Glavlit was not much of a story. After the end of the Doctors' Plot, she was finally able to join the Party. Then, after Khrushchev launched the battle against the cult of Stalin in 1956, the leadership of Glavlit changed, its ranks were purged, and she was sacked for knitting at a trade-union meeting. She had never knitted a thing in her life: someone had just been trying to teach her.

In time, she began to translate books: travel and exploration, Roald Amundsen and Jacques Cousteau. Now, at seventy-eight, she makes a living translating romantic novels. She consults me about the names of car parts and sometimes on some of the raunchier terminology.

What can I tell you about my other grandmother—Ester, Baba Tusya to me? First, that she was brave enough to refuse to cooperate with the secret police. Second, that she accepted a job with the secret police. Baba Tusya spent the early war years in Siberia with her mother who was exiled for 'religious propaganda' (though her mother was an atheist). For months Tusya dodged the regular attempts by a certain captain in the NKVD (the People's Committee for Internal Affairs) to draft her as an informer. The captain was, it seems, attracted to her. Perhaps this is why he did not beat her when he had her detained every few weeks. Nor did he carry out his threats to shoot her right then and there with the gun in his hand. At those times when she came close to signing, she thought of her mother—how would she look her in the eye?—and she refused. No, she did not think of what would happen to her mother if she died. She was nineteen.

Then a young man, a decorated disabled war veteran, swept in, put the NKVD captain in his place, and swept Tusya away to Moscow, where she returned to university and gave birth to a son.

She graduated in 1948, just as the Anti-Cosmopolitan Campaign was nearing full swing. 'This was before the killer doctors, but it was already at a point that makes me sick remembering. In any case, there was no place that would hire Jews.' She made the rounds for five months. Old teachers phoned her with leads, and she followed them up with ever decreasing hope. The same scenario unfolded again and again. 'You see, I don't have the typical looks, that is, not everyone can tell right off that I'm Jewish—so the way it usually worked was that my future immediate superior would happily tell me I was hired, and then the personnel department would not let me through after I filled out the application form.' The application form included a line marked 'ethnicity' (often it still does). The jobs she did not get:

a Latin teacher in a teacher's college; a cataloguer of war-trophy books at the Lenin Library; a librarian at the Library of Foreign Literature; a librarian anywhere; anything at all.

Then, finally, a stroke of luck: someone called to say that the Jewish Anti-Fascist Committee (JAFC) was looking to hire an administrative assistant who knew Hebrew. Now the JAFC had to be the one place left in town that would still hire a Jew. And, since Hebrew had not been taught in Russia since 1917, there could not be very many potential administrative assistants. Baba Tusya had grown up in Poland, in a Zionist family, with Hebrew as her first language. 'I ran, I literally ran to this Jewish Anti-Fascist Committee, which was on Kropotkin Street. They tested me. I translated right off the page. I filled out an application form. They had no personnel department. They offered it to me on the spot, with a very good salary, something like 150 roubles a month. That was on a Wednesday or a Thursday, and I was to report for work on Monday.'

It was October 1948. She reported for work on Monday and came face to face with a young man in an NKVD uniform guarding the sealed door to what had been the Jewish Anti-Fascist Committee. It was no longer. Its leadership had been arrested. They would be tried on espionage charges, and some of them would be killed. It was a stroke of luck, really, that she had not yet started work.

Not that she was thinking about that. Or about the fact that she might still be arrested: there was, after all, a record of her hiring that had been seized along with all the other JAFC papers. She was hysterical, she says. She was job-hunting again, with less hope than ever. She had an elderly mother, a son who was not yet four, and a husband who did not make much money. Her mother had once complained to a paediatrician that the boy's eyes showed 'two thousand years of the Jewish people's sorrow'. At his age, the doctor responded, 'Jewish sorrow can only be caused by malnutrition.'

And then my grandmother got a summons. A phone call, actually, but at that time people could be arrested in many different ways: any time of the day or night, by a single person or a squad, taken away by foot, by car, by bread truck. They telephoned to tell her to report to Lubyanka, the headquarters of the secret police, at ten on the following day.

Everyone cried, no one slept, and her husband promised to raise the boy and care for her mother. They packed the usual basket: dried bread, sugar, soap, a sweater and a change of underwear. She had forgotten all about the JAFC; she thought she was being arrested for the congratulatory telegram she had sent to a Zionist organization in Warsaw on the occasion of the founding of the state of Israel. Decades later, she would learn that hers was the only telegram sent by a private individual from the USSR. She had been unable to restrain herself.

'So I take my basket and go to Lubyanka—oh, pardon me, at that time it was called Dzerzhinsky Square. I go to the entrance door they told me to go to. The guard looks in my bag, laughs like it's very funny, and says, "Young lady, people with these bags go through the other door. But that's all right. Leave it here so you can pick it up when you leave." He calls on the telephone and says, "Someone will take you to Major Ivanova's office."'

The summons—the phone call—was a stroke of luck.

'So they take me to this woman. I was just a girl then—how old was I?—twenty-five. And here is a woman of about forty who greets me ever so nicely. She offers me a seat, and, shivering, I sit down. And she tells me they want to offer me a job, the position of a translator from Hebrew. I am in shock.'

It was a simple proposition. The state of Israel had just been formed, and the Soviet Union had been the first country to recognize it. There was suddenly official and unofficial international communication in Hebrew, and the Soviet secret police did not have a single staff member who knew Hebrew. The Jewish Anti-Fascist Committee's records had been seized when its leadership was arrested, and among these records was an application form filled out by a certain Ester Gessen, twenty-five, who knew Hebrew.

Major Ivanova, meanwhile, kept talking. 'She was painting a rosy picture of my future. I would have flexible hours. I would not have enough work to last an entire work day and I wouldn't have to sit there in the office. The pay would be even better than at the Anti-Fascist Committee, and I would have the rank of lieutenant right off. And before long I would be a major.

'I told her I'd have to consult my family. And that I would give her an answer tomorrow, and that I would come at the same time the following day but that now I had to run home. And she said, "Yes, of course, I understand," and she even made a joke, "Everyone must have got scared when we summoned you here." And I said, "Yes, and they are still terrified, and I want to go tell them I'm fine." And I went home, where I was received as though I'd just come back from the dead.'

She accepted the job.

I ought to be able to pause to explore the agony of the decision. How did a girl who had risked everything to resist cooperating with the secret police decide, in a matter of hours, to become its lieutenant? I'm afraid it's all very simple. It is better to have a lieutenant for a mother, a daughter, a wife, than not to have the mother, the daughter, the wife. It is better to work and to eat than to despair and count kopeks and be embarrassed by paediatricians.

'My God, we won't be able to say a word in the house any more!' Tusya's mother-in-law exclaimed.

'We knew we'd lose most of our friends,' Baba Tusya explains. 'No, not because they'd deplore the decision but because they'd be frightened. But then I consoled myself with the idea that I would just be translating.'

Major Ivanova's patience lasted until the evening, when she phoned, and Tusya accepted the job.

The next day she spent an hour filling out a book-length application form. Major Ivanova clickety-clicked into another room and returned a few minutes later with the words, 'Congratulations! You have been hired. Now only the medical examination is left.' Off she marched to the NKVD clinic.

'There have been few times in my life when I experienced such spiteful satisfaction. It had clearly been years since a Jew had come in for a medical examination at the NKVD clinic. And here I was, Ester Gessen, and you can imagine: the entire clinic was chasing around after me, dying to know what my position would be. And I assumed a proud pose and said, "It is a state secret, which I cannot disclose."'

Baba Tusya tends to forget that she is blind in one eye. Indeed, Major Ivanova had asked whether she had any health problems: Major Ivanova wanted Ester Gessen so badly she would have been willing to fix any problems raised by the clinic in advance. But my grandmother always forgets that she is blind in one eye, and she forgot to tell Major Ivanova. The major was beside herself when the last doctor on the medical committee, an optometrist, ruled my grandmother unsuitable for service. Ivanova extracted a promise from Tusya that she would return six months later, when the records of the medical examination had been destroyed, and try again.

'And I went home. I can't say that I was devastated. I was sad because I'd already got my expectations up. But then I thought, maybe it was a stroke of luck. And maybe I shouldn't go to work for the NKVD. Maybe we'd just manage somehow.'

Before the six months were up, Tusya got a job with a new Polish-language journal where she worked until she retired more than forty years later. Major Ivanova was devastated.

What else can I tell you about Baba Ruzya and Baba Tusya? First, that they have been best friends since 1950. Second, that they are colleagues as translators. Third, that they seem to hold conflicting opinions on everything, with the possible exception of a single traditional toast, pronounced at the end of an evening. It goes like this: 'May they all croak.' Meaning *them*—Comrade Stalin and all the other comrade monsters.

The obvious questions remain: where do crimes begin and end, and who, decades later, can be held responsible?

As I write this, my world, the world for which I returned from the United States, the world in which I reinvented myself as a Russian journalist just as the rest of the country was reinventing itself—this world is tumbling down. The *others* are coming back, may they all croak, and I know why this is. It is because we did not expose them, we did not try them, we did not judge them. We did not enumerate their crimes, and we did not say where they started and ended.

I know why this is. We all have our grandmothers. Merely by asking such questions each one of us risks betraying someone we love.

□

GRANTA

THE LAST EIGHTEEN DROPS

Vitali Vitaliev

Drinking vodka is just a memory for me now. Vodka was hurting me. I gave it up after I moved from Moscow to London (the move helped). Now I drink strong coffee, cup after cup, and remain nervously sensible to the reality around me: the avenue where I live in Muswell Hill, my small office in Islington, the bus journey in between. Sometimes I see huddles of men and women sitting on the street and sharing cans of extra-strong beer, bottles of fortified wine and cider. Sad types with broken lives. I think then of my days in the Soviet Union. My memories of vodka are rich and…I was going to write 'sweet', but that would not be quite the right word.

Burned to death with vodka

I was lucky to be born and brought up in a non-drinking family. A teetotal family in the Soviet Union was as rare then as a family without a television set would be now in Britain. From early childhood I was aware of the strange world of vodka and *pianie* (drunks) which surrounded us. I grew used to the sight of swaggering, foul-smelling and gibbering men in the streets and on buses and trains. I knew that the burly, loud-mouthed fellow who used to wander into the courtyard of our block of flats every morning to buy old rags from housewives was drunk. At least, my grandmother told me so. *'Staari v-e-e-shchee-ee pa-a-kupayem!'* ('We buy old clothes!') he would chant in a thick baritone. I was slightly afraid of him.

Playing with the other children in our block of flats, I was often chosen to impersonate the drunken head of the family who returns from work legless and is scolded by his wife—a common occurrence in many real-life families, as we well knew. I would stumble, fall down and give out incoherent yells from time to time. I enjoyed playing the drunk, perhaps because it was so far from my experience at home.

The only times a bottle of vodka would appear on our family table were during the infrequent visits of my father's uncle Pavel, who lived in Dnepropetrovsk and was a colonel in the Soviet Army. I liked his visits. After a couple of shots he would become facetious and tell funny stories about his army life, and I enjoyed the sight of his rough military tunic hanging on the clothes rack in the corridor next to my father's raincoat. It smelled of war and adventure. When Uncle Pavel was in a particularly good mood (usually after three or four shots of vodka), he would even allow me to play with his cockaded service-cap.

It wasn't until I was about seven that I realized how dangerous, even lethal, vodka could be. My parents told me that a young man who lived in the neighbouring block of flats, and whom I had often seen playing dominoes on the battered wooden table in our courtyard, had died. When I asked my grandmother why, she made a serious face and mumbled: *'Zgorel ot vodki'* (literally: 'He burned himself to death with vodka'). It was hard for me to imagine how a plain, water-like liquid could kill (let alone burn to death) someone so big and strong. I remember peeping—with the other kids—into the basement flat where the domino player lay in state, covered with wreaths and fir-tree branches. His father—an old man, who had drunk vodka with his son but had survived—shooed us away.

Yevgeny Bulavin

When I was sixteen, in the summer holidays before my final year at school, I went with a classmate to a sports camp near the village of Gaidary. The camp was in desperate need of kitchen staff, and we volunteered to work as dishwashers in the canteen.

It was here that I met Yevgeny Bulavin. He was a second-year student of physical culture, and at eighteen, he was almost a patriarch in our eyes. He was also an alcoholic, but we didn't realize it then. We were eager to imitate him. We would finish washing-up after dinner at around eleven p.m. Then, under Yevgeny's expert guidance, we would scour the camp in search of something to drink. This is how, for the first and last time in my life, I came to drink perfume. It was called 'Russian Forest' and when we diluted it with water, the opaque liquid in each glass rose with a soapy foam. For the rest of the evening, we stank like three walking barber's shops.

Few things in life were capable of making Yevgeny as distraught as he was at the sight of an empty vodka bottle. Having placed the 'dead' bottle horizontally on the table, like a perished soldier laid to rest by his comrade-in-arms, he would watch it closely, trying to hypnotize it into filling up with vodka again. His theory was that no matter how empty the bottle might seem, there would always be eighteen drops of vodka left in it. After several minutes of silent grieving he would lift the bottle from the table, turn it upside down, and shake it over a glass. Miraculously, eighteen indolent vodka drops would indeed slide from its neck, one after another. Not sixteen, not nineteen, but invariably eighteen. You can check it yourself. Some abstruse physical law is hiding inside those empty bottles.

He was a sportsman, a home-grown philosopher, a draft dodger (he simulated dromomania, an irrepressible passion for purposeless travel) and, I suppose, my drinking supervisor. His favourite toast was 'To this glass not being the last one, to more frequent drinking—long live alcohol—hooray!' Passing a drunkard lying in the gutter, he would say: 'Happy guy! Look, he is already enjoying himself, and we haven't drunk anything yet!'

Yevgeny's favourite haunt was the shabby hut of the village home-brewer known throughout the area as 'Baba Lena' (Granny Lena). She produced *samogon*—a stinking potato spirit—on an almost industrial basis. Home-brewing in the Soviet Union was a serious criminal offence, but Baba Lena was ingenious. She would post her old husband, shrunk from decades of heavy drinking, at the front gate. 'Speak up: I can't hear you!' he would mutter to visitors, as he studied them with the eyes of a cunning Ukrainian peasant. Then he would yell, without turning his head: 'Lena! Have we got anything left?' From inside a nearby shed, a woman's voice would echo in Ukrainian: 'Yeah. Just a tiny bit. Have they got an empty container?'

And then you would hear the hissing and rattling sounds of their sophisticated moonshine machinery starting up.

It was not long before we were blacklisted by the cautious Baba Lena. It happened after Yevgeny tried (unsuccessfully) to catch one of her chickens to diversify our camp diet. Eventually, Baba Lena herself was arrested and sent to prison as a 'threat to the law and order of the whole of the Severski Donets region', as a local newspaper put it.

The shoe-polish sandwich

Three years later, as a second-year university student, I took a summer job as a sleeping-car attendant. Each railway carriage had two attendants working alternate shifts. My fellow worker, Mitrich, was an old man with an amazing capacity for vodka. He drank two half-litre bottles three times a day, locking himself in his compartment and gulping each dose down within the space of five to ten minutes. Then he would attend to his chores: checking tickets, sweeping the carriage floors and taking small bribes (usually in the form of vodka) from stowaways. A litre of vodka didn't have much effect on him, though his normally expressionless eyes would start gleaming. 'Wine is bad for you, but vodka is very healthy,' he would say. 'Doctors recommend it.'

Officially, the railway was a no-drinking zone. But this did not inhibit the staff on our train. The chief attendant would routinely ransack the compartments of his subordinates in search of a drink and would confiscate (and consume) anything with an alcohol content: vodka, beer, perfume, shampoo, toothpaste or even shoe polish, which he used to spread on a slice of bread (shoe-polish sandwiches were supposed to give you a mildly inebriated feeling—I didn't try one myself).

One night, when I was on duty in carriage thirteen, smoking a cheap Cuban cigar so as not to fall asleep, I had a visit from the engine driver himself. He was eager to share a bottle of vodka with me. I could see that he was already so stoned he could hardly walk. All the while, the train kept roaring along. The driver explained that he had left the engine on 'autopilot' as there were no scheduled stops for the next 200 kilometres. He also assured me that his young assistant was still in the driver's cabin, just in case, although the latter was apparently so drunk that he couldn't stand either. It took a considerable effort—mental and physical—to persuade the driver to return to his post.

On our train's forty-eight-hour journey from the Black Sea coast to the Baltic, there was only one station which had a vodka shop in the vicinity. The train stopped there for only ten minutes. An hour before the vodka stop, Mitrich would become agitated. As the train approached the station, he would stand on a footboard with an empty pillowcase in his hand. Then he would leap off while the train was still moving, and race to the vodka shop. Ten minutes was barely long enough, and he would usually jump back on to the train when it was already sliding along the platform. Several vodka bottles would be jingling amicably inside the pillowcase.

Since my father was a nuclear physicist, he was allocated pure alcohol for cleaning the optical instruments at his office. What he didn't use he would bring home. My father kept the alcohol in an unlocked cupboard, where it was soon discovered by Yevgeny Bulavin, who had become a frequent guest at the flat after our dishwashing stint. 'Your father's optical equipment won't suffer if the liquid is not exactly ninety-six per cent proof,' said my drinking tutor. So one day, when my father was at work, we poured out half of the spirit and topped the bottle up with tap water. We drank the alcohol straight off, on the balcony. It was like swallowing a ball of fire. The alcohol had to be washed down immediately with water to avoid burning your intestines. One of the nastiest tricks played on me by Yevgeny was to offer me another glass of the spirit as a chaser, instead of water. I nearly choked to death.

Mine's a large tooth-powder

Later, I drank more routinely, in Moscow drinking sessions with my friends: a bottle of vodka in the centre of the table, and the telephone covered with a cushion—the KGB's bugs were everywhere—to give us a naive illusion of privacy.

Drinking under Communism was not hedonistic. It provided us with an outlet—a coveted, even if short-term, escape from political dogma and social gloom. A bottle of vodka was therefore a sort of liquid hard currency, much more reliable (and much more stable) than money. Anything, from a trip abroad to difficult-to-obtain roof tiles, could be bought and sold for alcohol, and had its inflation-proof vodka equivalent.

But at the end of the 1980s Mikhail Gorbachev attempted to curb his country's near-endemic alcoholism. Countless sobriety societies, which every worker was forced to join (fees were simply deducted from salaries), sprang up like mushrooms after a good July rain. These societies were staffed for the most part by carefully vetted bureaucrats from the uneven ranks of heavy drinkers and chronic alcoholics. They did nothing apart from organizing politically correct 'sober' birthday parties and wedding ceremonies, during which vodka was covertly poured from samovars and kettles. Alcohol was hard to find in the shops. The effect was predictable: vodka-deprived drunks took to shampoo, glue, perfume, insect repellent and window cleaner. In a Moscow park, I once saw three drunks boiling tooth powder in an empty can on top of a bonfire. They boiled it for five hours (or so they said), then carefully removed the alcohol from the top with tablespoons, drank it—and immediately started vomiting.

Vodka came back in a flood after Gorbachev went. Westerners assumed that with the collapse of Communism, people in the former Soviet Union would drink less—a democratic society would provide alternative forms of escape: books, a free media, foreign travel, the cornucopia of consumer goods. The reality has been different. Drinking in the post-Communist world has increased dramatically since the fall of the Berlin Wall.

How to drink it

Few Russian phenomena are quite so distorted and misunderstood in the West as vodka. In a recent James Bond movie I was appalled to see Robbie Coltrane, in the role of a Russian Mafioso, holding vodka in his mouth before swallowing it. And the Russian General was taking little swigs of vodka from a pocket flask.

Such solecisms suggest a complete lack of understanding of vodka's qualities as a drink and of its social significance. A little history: vodka first appeared in Poland (and then in Russia) as a medicine. It was noticed that the water in wine or beer left outside in winter would freeze, leaving a higher-strength alcohol residue. People started using this residue externally, to treat cuts, and, in ointment form, to soothe aching joints. When the mass production of vodka began in Poland in the fifteenth century, it started to be taken through the mouth, in spoonfuls, for bad colds and dodgy stomachs.

Only in the eighteenth century did vodka begin to be drunk for pleasure. But, though the motive for drinking it had changed, the method of drinking it did not. Medicine isn't drunk to be savoured, after all; you swallow it down in one gulp, wash it down with water, and wait for the healing effects to begin.

This medicinal approach has remained largely unchanged since the fifteenth century, even if the range of ailments has broadened to include psychological conditions such as the inability to cope with an oppressive reality, the desire for escape from the hardships of life, the failure to relax in a social situation, and so on.

As a thoroughly filtered product of distillation, a good vodka is designed to be the purest alcoholic drink on earth. Any additives, even ice cubes, immediately ruin its character. Flavoured vodkas, which are increasingly popular in the West, are a corruption of the drink's very nature. My heart aches whenever I see London pub-goers cheerfully mixing vodka with lime, orange juice or Coca-Cola. It also aches whenever I watch a film in which a Russian smashes his vodka glass against a wall after emptying it. The truth is that glass is too precious a commodity to be disposed of in such a barbaric way. A glass is more than important—it is indispensable. This too is partly because of vodka's medicinal roots. Would you swig cough mixture from a bottle? Would you sip your anti-indigestion (or anti-constipation) medicine from a flask? No. You need a proper glass, which makes it easier, faster and less unpleasant. A Russian vodka-drinker will give anything for a glass. Only the most degraded of alcoholics would drink vodka straight from the bottle. It would be like severing the last remaining connection with civilized humanity.

Here is an illustration.

The minister goes thirsty

In the late Eighties, I was sent to Belarus by *Krokodil* magazine to write a 'rosy' piece glorifying the republic's achievements in procuring food for its population when the rest of the country was starving.

There was indeed food in Belarus's shops (I remember being particularly impressed by the availability of two different sorts of cheese, when the shops in Moscow remained totally cheese-less). Throughout my trip I was accompanied by the republic's Minister of Agriculture. We travelled in his chauffeured black Volga limo.

On the last day, the Minister became restless and agitated. He was looking around himself like a troubled bird, and kept winking at me conspiratorially from the front seat of the Volga (Yevgeny Bulavin used to call this condition 'the state of pre-drinking exaltation'). At last, after a visit to a collective farm, he leaned towards me and whispered: 'Vitali Vladimirovich, do you feel like having some rest?'

I knew that this was a euphemism for having a drink. On my journalistic missions I had to be careful not to fall into the trap of drinking with the potential subjects of my satirical pieces, who were only waiting for a chance to compromise me and ruin my credibility. I remember one bureaucrat in the Zaporozhie region following me around with a string bag full of booze, whining 'Let's have a drink, Vitali Vladimirovich.' I refused to be provoked: a written denunciation, substantiated with photos of me drinking, would have reached Moscow before I did.

But this case was different: the article was a positive one. There was no immediate danger in drinking with the Minister, except for the hazard of being caught doing so in a public place (like a restaurant), in which case even he would have lost his ministerial job. (A popular joke of those times concerned a director preparing to make love to his secretary in his office. 'Have you closed the door?' she asks. 'What for?' he replies. 'We're not drinking, are we?')

So I agreed to have a drink with the hospitable Minister, and suggested that we should do so in the privacy of my hotel room. 'Are you mad?' the Minister objected. He told me that stooges hung around the hotel night and day. When they spotted a group of men with carefully wrapped parcels entering the building, they would wait for half an hour, and then burst into their room without knocking. If they saw the men drinking, they would blackmail them. Normally people would pay up rather than risk exposure: a hotel room was also classified as a public place.

Having stuffed the Volga boot with booze, we headed for a nearby forest, where the minister thought we would be safe. It was late November. For a good hour we drove along a narrow forest path in complete darkness. The forests are thick in Belarus. During the Second World War they gave excellent shelter to the partisans, and the Nazis were scared of entering them. But we were neither Nazis nor partisans. We simply wanted a drink.

'Can't we stop here? It looks perfectly safe,' I kept saying, like a tired child in the back of a car. 'No, it's not safe enough,' the Minister would reply. We spoke in whispers.

Finally, we reached the end of the forest path. The car could go no further. We could hear wolves howling behind the bushes.

'It's OK,' the Minister said to his driver. We climbed out of the car. The driver switched on the headlights and started laying out the food and vodka on the boot. When everything was ready and we were about to have some 'rest', it turned out that we had no glasses.

On the way back, none of us uttered a word. We could hear the vodka bottles clinking in the boot, as if they were giggling at us.

Avoid...

Another Western misconception about vodka concerns the names given to some popular brands. In any London off-licence you can find cheap locally made vodkas with names like *Vladivar, Imperial Commissar,* or even *Tolstoy*. Now, *Vladivar* would be a fine name for a beer (*var* comes from the verb *varit*—to brew), but for a vodka, which is distilled rather than brewed, it is ridiculous. *Imperial Commissar* is a plain contradiction in itself—like a four-angled triangle, or a 'royal proletarian'. As for poor Leo Tolstoy, a confirmed teetotaller, vegetarian and a tireless propagandist of abstention, to name a vodka after him is like naming a beefburger after Gandhi.

I would not touch them. I would rather go for the obscure Luxembourg-made brand *Black Death*, or for the Danish liqueur *North Sea Oil*. Then at least you know what you are in for.

The placebo

The most memorable of the alcoholics I have met was Eduard Drozdov, the chief narcologist of Moscow in the late Eighties. Narcology is a branch of medicine dealing with addiction, and in Russia it is associated primarily with the treatment of heavy drinkers.

In 1986 when I was working as a special correspondent for *Krokodil* in Moscow, I received a letter complaining that a vodka shop was operating in the grounds of the city's biggest narcological clinic, where several thousand alcoholics were undergoing treatment. When I went to investigate I found, to my astonishment, that a small vodka shop was indeed doing a brisk trade. The patients would lower a bucket containing a bundle of roubles from the hospital windows, and winch up their vodka.

Eduard Drozdov was the hospital's head physician—as well as being a city council deputy, and a Hero of Socialist Labour. The professor expressed his horror at what I had learned, and promised to attend to this 'scandalous breach of regulations' as soon as he had a spare moment. Unfortunately, though, his diary was full for days ahead. To prove how busy he was, he invited me to spend some time in his office while he received his visitors and patients.

From a cosy armchair in the corner of his spacious study, I watched as a succession of grief-stricken wives, mothers and sisters of alcoholics passed through. The women cried, told heartbreaking stories and pleaded with Drozdov to save their drink-sodden husbands, sons and brothers. He tried to calm them down, and gave each of them a packet containing a 'miracle drug' which, he said, might help their beloveds. Before leaving his office, each woman put a carefully wrapped parcel on his desk, which Drozdov locked away in his office safe, still wrapped. Watching the women was the best anti-alcoholism propaganda one could imagine, and by the end of the day I had sworn to give up drinking myself—starting the following morning.

But Drozdov himself was much less affected. At exactly six p.m., when the door closed behind the last weeping woman, a young long-legged nurse danced into the office. 'Well, Edik,' she said, 'what have we got in the takings tonight?' Without asking for the narcologist's permission she opened his safe, took out several of the parcels left by the women, and unwrapped them. They contained bottles of drink.

'What shall we have?' she said. 'Napoleon cognac? Possolskaya Vodka? Whisky from Scotland?'

'Hush, Lyuba, there's a journalist here,' said Drozdov.

'So what?' giggled Lyuba. 'With your reputation and your party record, you have nothing to worry about.'

She was right: the chances that the vigilant censors would allow into print a story about Moscow's chief narcologist and a high-ranking member of the Soviet establishment taking bribes in the form of booze were less than zero.

'Hey, journalist, will you have a drink with us?' Lyuba asked, winking at me mischievously.

Three hours later we were still there, finishing off the third (or was it the fourth?) bottle. The chief narcologist was extremely drunk. 'This is narcology in action for you, Vitali,' he was saying. 'We are not simply drinking here. We are ex-pe-ri-men-ting! This is your first lesson in self-applied narcology. Like all pioneering physicians, we are testing the effects of the drug—courageously—on ourselves!'

He produced a white pill from his pocket. 'Take it! It will kill the smell of booze, and your wife won't suspect a thing!'

'What sort of pills were you giving to the visitors?' I asked him.

'Ha! You won't believe it, but they were simple mints. Alcoholism is incurable, but my theory is that you can affect a patient psychologically, if he believes that he is taking a powerful anti-drinking drug.'

I could hardly take any more alcohol, or any more Drozdov, for that matter.

'Look, Vitali, can you do me a favour and forget about the vodka shop?' he asked me suddenly. 'Leave it alone. Let it operate. I don't want to spoil my relationship with the local council.'

'I can't promise anything,' I said and stood up to leave.

'They won't allow you to publish the story anyway!' Drozdov shouted as I walked away.

Needless to say, my wife smelled the booze before I had even unlocked the door of my flat. In this respect, Drozdov's pioneering experiment proved a failure.

He was right about the fate of my story, however. Next morning, my editor received a phone call from the Communist Party Central Committee. We were forbidden to publish or even to consider for publication anything connected with the narcological clinic or with the highly respected Professor Drozdov.

In the following years, I often saw the chief narcologist on television and heard him on the radio. He spoke about the dangers of alcoholism, and called for complete and total sobriety.

Never another drop

I remember a Moscow colleague of mine, a gifted journalist, who was suffering from a bleeding stomach ulcer, but kept drinking vodka, washing it down with Almagel—a sickeningly sweet liquid medicine. 'What are you doing? You are killing yourself,' I told him once as he coughed up blood after another glass of vodka. 'I don't care if I die tomorrow,' he replied, swallowing a spoonful of Almagel. 'I don't care whether I survive for another twenty years of queuing and humiliation. I don't like this life. Do you?'

What could I say? By that time, like most of my friends, I had a duodenal ulcer myself. A bottle of Almagel would routinely stand in the middle of the table during our friendly get-togethers. Next to a bottle of vodka, of course. Such was the cycle of our Soviet existence. It seemed that only death or vodka could break it. It wasn't until years later, in London, that I gave up alcohol altogether, and returned to my teetotal roots.

As for Yevgeny Bulavin, he was thrown out of the Physical Culture Institute for excessive drinking and took a job in a milk-processing plant. The main perk was that he could drink as much milk as he wanted. When I last saw him, he said he was consuming up to twenty litres a day. He felt that ten litres of milk on an empty stomach had the same effect on the brain as one glass of vodka. I doubted it, but said nothing. One never knew with Yevgeny. □

GRANTA

PANORAMA
John Ranard

The Baltic Coast, Kaliningrad, 1998

Sokolniki Park, Moscow, 1998

Outdoor ballroom dancing in Sokolniki Park, Moscow, 1998

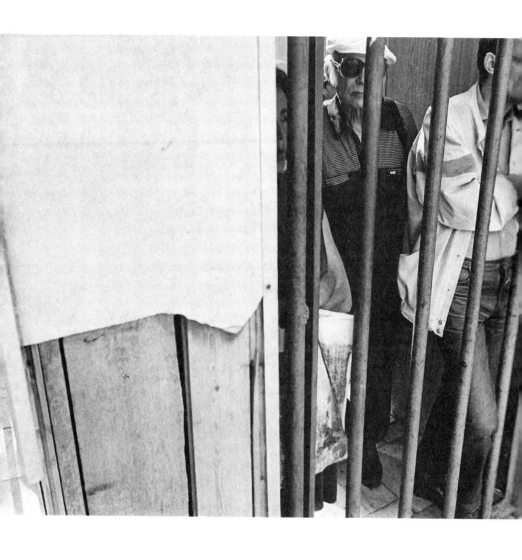

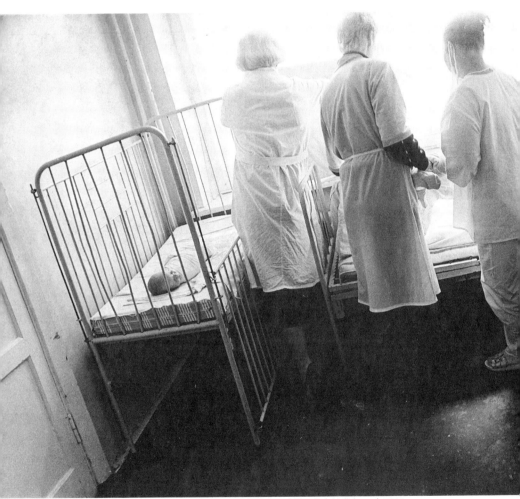

Orphaned HIV positive newborns in Kaliningradsky General Hospital, Kaliningrad, 1998

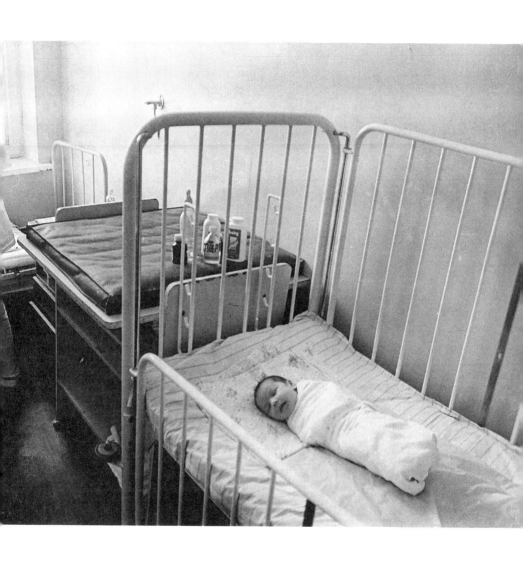

Drugs raid, Kaliningrad, 1998

Travelling funfair, Kaliningrad, 1998

Ballroom dancing workshop in the Palace of Youth, Kaliningrad, 1998

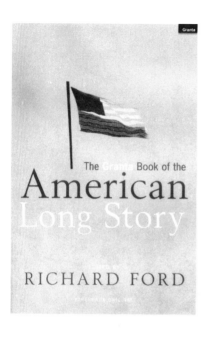

GRANTA

PETER TRUTH
Charlotte Hobson

Petya Pravda's dead. He died forty days ago, as elongated and translucent as an icon. His mother found him in the morning, and straight away set up a wail that brought in the neighbours: Pyotr! Petya! My little Petya! And they hurried in, old Kolya hitching up his belly, stinking of hangover, Maria Nikolaevna already back from the market, and my landlady, Sveta, wrapped in her dressing gown with emerald eyeshadow on one eye.

It wasn't the first time they'd come running to this cry—Petya's come close to the brink a few times during the last couple of years. More than once, Kolya has dashed off to the doctor while Sveta tremblingly applied the first aid she learned at the factory and Petya lay so pale it seemed the colour had left even his irises. At last he'd blink and all the women would start laughing and crying. Sveta would wipe off with her thumb the crimson ring of lipstick she had planted on his mouth. And Petya would just lie there and, after a few moments, turn on his side and close his eyes.

But this time he stopped breathing during the night, and by morning there was nothing they could do. His mother, who is almost crippled by arthritis, was persuaded to rest. Kolya closed Petya's eyes with fifty-kopek pieces, and the women organized the funeral. By the time I saw him he was stretched out on the sofa and surrounded by crosses and incense. I thought how amused he would have been at being given an Orthodox send-off—yet, in a way, it wasn't inappropriate.

Pyotr Pravda—Peter Truth. Sometimes I felt part of the burden of life that Petya found repellent was his name—how to live up to such a name! The first Pyotr Pravda, his grandfather, a railway worker who fought in the civil war, had taken the surname as a new beginning in a brand-new world. A black-and-white photograph of him hung in their front room—a bony face with dark eyes, a medal-decked chest and a Soviet passport, touched up with red ink, poking out of his top pocket. Petya looked identical, though not as proud. His mother got him to hang up the photo not so long ago. 'There,' she said. 'I only knew him when he came back from the camps, like a little old nut and grumpy as hell. May he rest in peace.'

His grandfather's truth had aged by the time Petya inherited it. Not that it bothered him either way at first, of course. The fat little Petya of early photographs, stiff as an overstuffed bear in six layers of artificial fur, holding the string of a toboggan and beaming as hard as his chubby, chilly face would allow—he was no child philosopher.

Perhaps the shadow that crept over him was particular to his experience—vodka in the courtyard at fifteen, his jaw broken by the tough guys on military service, then a two-room flat with an invalid mother and his father a sodden drunk in the next province. And Friday evenings in small-town Russia, a pack of young boys bursting with energy and nowhere to expend it. By the early Nineties, when Petya was a student, the truth was a sordid, dirty little rag. No kind of word to have on your identity card.

When I first met Petya, we were both at university. He was too thin, with a face like a little boy, and he wore the same threadbare jacket summer and winter. He and a gang of friends were known as the Narcomen and spent their nights and most of their days talking, drinking and talking. The exams, when the time came, were oral—no problem. I sat in on an exam of Petya's, once. I'd been up all night with the Narcomen when he decided I must go with him as his talisman. It was the sort of joke he loved.

Petya's mother kept every bit of paper, including the doctor's notes from when her illness was not so advanced. So the next day we arrived at the faculty together and presented the lecturer with a note stating that P. Pravda had arthritic cramps in the neck and shoulder area, and three days' bed-rest was essential. The professor, Maria Mikhailovna, was a motherly figure well known for her susceptibility to young men, but even she raised her eyebrows as Petya assured her that he wasn't about to miss this exam for the world—'to lose a chance to defend my Pushkin would set me back even further, Maria Mikhailovna. You understand me.' He fixed her with his dark eyes. 'But Charlotte has agreed to massage the area during the exam, if you don't object.' And I stood behind him and rubbed his neck.

'Pushkin massages his words into place...' Petya began, making me snort. He continued smoothly. 'Even the clumsiest, most unmanageable Russian verb, stiff with prefixes and trailing an endless, glutinous reflexive agreement, is made to feel supple and extraordinarily powerful...because each of them occupies an

unassailable position in Pushkin's world, in the world of language, a world that is lucid and vivid, ordered and yet more spontaneous than our own—a world that, in fact, is more real than reality...'
Maria Mikhailovna smiled dreamily and marked him 'excellent'.

All the Narcomen were bright—Citrus, the performance artist, Vlad, the theatre designer, Zossya, a writer who had a job as a nightwatchman in a home for the deaf and dumb, Sergei, who translated Latin American literature. They rolled joints on the photo of old Pyotr Pravda and discussed their enthusiasms night after night. Yet they were convinced that brains were no use to them in their Russia. 'What's the point?' they said to me. 'To be successful, you need connections or you need to be a thug. You don't need brains.'

It made me angry. 'But how can you say so? Maybe under Brezhnev it was true, but now there is every opportunity! You can work, write, start a business, be free...'

'Oh yes?' Vlad, I think it was, glanced at me coolly. 'For a moment drop your Western assumption that elections and a free press mean democracy, which is the solution to all social ills, and look. Free thought? I've had that all my life. Of course there was a shortage of books, of music, before, but we passed them around, we got hold of things. We had less, but we appreciated it more. Travel? In the old days we could travel, spend the summer in Dubrovnik, sail on Lake Baikal, walk in Karelia. A ticket to Moscow cost seven roubles then—now it's 25,000. I couldn't afford to go up to Moscow for a week, let alone look for a job there, rent a flat, buy a suit... Start a business? Just look at the kind of guys running businesses down here in Voronezh. Do you think it's a coincidence that they all look like apes? The only businesses that succeed in what they call this 'transitional period' are rackets. And I'm not interested.'

I felt chastened.

Soon after this, Petya was deemed unsuitable as a university student. The other professors didn't find him amusing. They wanted a display of the linguistic developments pioneered by Pushkin, a knowledge of the social background that gave rise to Pushkin's verse. The rest of the country might be going to pot, but here the old standards prevailed. Students still took classes in ideological enlightenment; boys spent Mondays wriggling across rough grass in camouflage, girls learned to assemble a Kalashnikov in fifteen seconds. As for ideology—for goodness' sake, the professors seemed to be saying, that's been dead since the Seventies. But it doesn't change the fact that the form and rituals of the language of historical determinism are still necessary to us. Anyway—look at him. He's quite plainly a degenerate.

Petya sat before them with a fixed smile and attempted to interest them in Buddhism. Nirvana, he suggested, was a civilized type of afterlife, a communist type, even. Then he went out and got drunk and had a fight with the doorman at the university buffet. He didn't go to court, but it was the end of his student days.

His mother wept and took it up with the bureaucrats, but she needed more than her invalid's pension to get their decision overturned. So instead she exchanged her father's medals for a wad of greasy roubles and booked Petya an appointment for an alcohol cure.

'Hmmm, been having a few too many, have you?' said the doctor cheerily. 'Your Mama's paid me in advance for the pleasure of fitting you with a capsule. You know how it works, don't you? A little container of poison under the skin of your arm. It sits there all snug, not causing you a moment's trouble until you have a few grams of alcohol. The casing partially dissolves, and *yolki palki!* you feel sick as a rabbit. Outcome: you stay off the stuff. How do you like the sound of that? You've got to be careful though, you can do yourself an injury if you go on a real binge.'

Petya looked faintly green. 'Listen, doctor. This is going to do me no good. My system won't take it. What do you say to splitting the cash and you get to keep the capsule?'

The doctor studied him for a minute, then measured his blood pressure. He checked Petya's reflexes and shone a light in his ears. 'Well...' he said at last. 'Sixty–forty, and you're on.'

I scarcely saw him that autumn. He slept a lot, grew thinner and older. Once or twice we stood outside his window and called 'Petya! *Praaavda!*' in a whisper and he appeared in his dressing gown. He sat with us outside and lit up a ready-rolled joint, his eyes huge, almond-shaped and expressionless.

How is a man to live? This was our subject, as we sat in the yard under the gaze of his black eyes. And while inflation raced and the post-Soviet world grew increasingly grotesque, Petya decided that the only sincere way to live was in the mind. He became a zealot. 'From henceforth I have decided to live by the seasons,' he announced to us. 'In the summer—alcohol. In autumn, the new harvest of grass. In the winter, fireworks and speed. And in the spring, all damp and tender— the only thing for it is opium.'

'Petya is a dualist, you understand,' Vlad said. 'He sees that freedom lies in the spirit, not the body. The demands of the world— to earn a living, to get a degree, to covet and desire and envy; there's no difference between them! They are all temptations that distract one from matters of the spirit. It's not Petya who's irresponsible. Quite the opposite—the irresponsible ones are those who devote their lives to their career and their family at the expense of their soul.'

Petya saw my face and laughed. 'Don't listen to this antisocial nonsense!' he said, and changed the subject. I never discovered whether Vlad was expressing Petya's ideas, or his own.

Alcohol was always there: vodka was the secondary currency after dollars—all government employees, workmen, policemen and university lecturers accepted it. On every corner, friends and strangers flung out their arms and said, 'Let's drink!' But it didn't satisfy Petya. 'In reality,' he used to say, 'I do not like these official intoxicants. They make you stupid and lustful.'

Autumn was a pleasant season. The import of cannabis was controlled by Zossya's deaf and dumb people. It was plentiful, cheap and good quality. But when the winter set in, month after month of dark, cold days, Petya needed to go faster. Then he'd try the university laboratories for amphetamines—he had an acquaintance there, a panda-eyed girl who'd help him out. It wasn't such a smooth journey, though. A couple of times her supplies gave Petya's mother a scare.

Finally, spring came, and with it heroin from Central Asia. I hadn't seen Petya for some time when a group of us went out to a dacha one April weekend. There was still slush on the ground, but the breeze was exhilarating, life was stirring in the woods. The others went on ahead. By the time I arrived they were all lying on the sofa smiling beatifically, apart from Petya, who stood beside me and looked them over.

'All of this free market, it's just as stupid as our Soviet materialism...' he began. 'Now the people think that they were wrong all these years to believe in communism, because it never gave them the glossy washing machines and American trainers that the free market has. But they don't understand. Any philosophy which has as its highest aim a state in which everyone has washing machines, whether it achieves that by collective effort or individual, is poor and mean. Do you see?'

'And what about your mother?' I meant—she needs you.

'My mother? She suffocates me with her preventative medicines, with her meals, her "eat up!", her obsession with the flesh. Everywhere it's the same. In the street—shops, posters, people shoving to get the last tin of pork, beggars—why don't they die? They'd be happier. Even in the Church it's all money, money, gold icons, fat priests, and people hoping their loathsome flesh will be preserved for eternity... It's disgusting.' He grinned at me. 'If only I were a religious man, how people would admire me!'

The Voronezh police didn't think much of Petya's theories. In fairness to them, they didn't think much at all. They arrested him one drunken summer evening and advised him that such a carry-on was bad for his health. To push the point home they broke a couple of his ribs and gave his kidneys a good bruising. His mother blanched and put him to bed, but he couldn't settle until he'd downed the Lily-of-the-Valley cologne he'd given her for International Women's Day.

The ribs healed, leaving Petya breathless, but apparently stronger than ever. Even when the snows began he wore the same ragged little jacket and trousers from which his thin bruised arms and feet protruded; his skin turned waxy yellow. He moved with jerky, horrible energy and he was always making plans. In the night he'd bang on my door to say, 'Let's go to Central Asia. In the spring. We'll study the way of the dervishes.'

Sveta, my landlady, said, 'He's not long for us.'

A couple of months ago the snow began to thaw and the litter that had stayed hidden all winter poked out of the slush. Spring had come again. And with it, according to Vlad, who was at the funeral, an especially pure load of heroin. Petya had been warned, Vlad said, and Petya, more than anyone, knew the score.

The funeral was a pitiful affair. It was cold and muddy and the mourners stood in a puddle as the coffin was lowered into the grave. Petya's mother couldn't afford the full Orthodox service; a deacon read the abbreviated version in a monotone and hurried back to his car.

Afterwards there was a wake back at the flat. We stood about feeling awkward until a few toasts were drunk—without clinking glasses, as is the custom when you drink to the dead. Slowly the atmosphere warmed up and the Narcomen, who had been looking forlorn, began to talk and gesticulate. Zossya, telling one of Petya's stories, knocked old Petya Pravda's picture off the wall on to the samovar, breaking the glass, and his grimaces of apology made everyone laugh. We stayed till midnight, by which time the flat was a mess of plates, and tears, and jokes, and empty bottles.

According to Orthodox custom, after death the soul remains in this world for forty days before departing to the next. So it was forty days later that we met to say goodbye to Petya Pravda.

It was less emotional than the funeral. Citrus was leaving for St Petersburg, and Petya's mother gave him some of Petya's books with a scolding to dress warmly. I watched her bustle about the flat and wondered about her arthritis.

'Yes,' she said and for the first time that day her eyes filled with tears. 'It is strange, but the flat has become so warm since…since… It used to be damp, the draughts gave me so much pain, but you know, I am a crazy old woman, but I think it is my son looking after me.'

The photograph of old Pyotr Pravda was in its old place, and without the glass, the resemblance to his grandson was even more marked. But after its dip in the samovar, it was looking its age. The red of the passport had made a bloody wound down his chest. Around his head was a yellow-brown tea stain, and his dark eyes gazed out of this impromptu halo, serene and yet despairing.   □

GRANTA

THE ROMANOVS COME TO STAY

Frances Welch

When I was a child I seemed to live in a fog of inattention which cleared only when I was alone. In company, my sight was a blur and my hearing a fuzz. Hands would wave in my face, 'Wake up!' Sometimes the tone was teasing and other times admonitory; neither had any effect.

The moment that the fog first cleared—or so I remember it—came on a family holiday in Norfolk. It was a summer's day. I see myself hanging awkwardly over a banister in our holiday home with my legs splayed and chest pressed hard against the wood. I am, as usual, half listening and half watching. A large black book is being passed between my father and brother. My father has adopted his lecturer's stance: poised, legs crossed, toes pointing outwards. He is wearing summer shorts and sandals. My brother Nick takes the book and flicks the pages in a desultory way. My father is telling him the story in the book.

The story is tragic. I catch the words 'shootings', and 'the whole family' and, most particularly, 'five children'. I go down the stairs quietly, anxious not to interrupt him. I want to look at the pictures, I want to know the whole story. My father, surprised by my appearance next to him, is nevertheless happy to rearrange his legs and direct his speech at me. He holds up photographs. The beauty of the children in them satisfactorily compounds my sense of tragedy.

The book that my father read from that day was Robert K. Massie's *Nicholas and Alexandra*, which culminates in the murder of the Tsar and Tsarina and their five children by Bolshevik guards. A cellar in Yekaterinburg, 17 July 1918. It had taken twenty minutes to kill them; the women had sewn jewels into their corsets, the bullets bounced off them, and the guards had eventually bayoneted their victims to death. I asked my father why it had happened. It seemed that the children had done nothing wrong. There had been an injustice. I felt a thrill of triumph in discovering proof that life was, as I had always suspected, essentially unfair and sad.

My first faltering steps out of the fog would have entailed getting hold of the book. I see myself devouring photographs and learning to tell the difference between the five children. Olga was the eldest and therefore, of course, the most sensible; the second daughter, Tatyana, was the prettiest, and the third, Maria, the slightly dumpy one; the youngest, Anastasia, was the jolliest and most attractive. Alexis was easy because he was the longed-for only son, the youngest. In one picture he wore a leg brace. He was—I discovered with relish a new and difficult word—a haemophiliac.

My spirits soared when I found the photograph of savage, sinister Rasputin. Here was a sorcerer possessed of miraculous healing powers who had cured the boy Alexis. I imitated his pose, with forefinger raised, in the mirror. And I memorized the details of his grisly murder: he was given enough poisoned pink cakes to kill ten men, he was shot at least four times; after all that, I would tell my schoolfriends, he actually died by drowning.

I was awarded *Nicholas and Alexandra* to take back to my boarding school. I would comb the class newspaper for anything related to the Romanovs and 'bags' it with a biro circle. I sellotaped corners of stiff paper on to the inside cover of the book; into these I slotted newspaper cuttings. The cuttings, in 1970, mostly related to the false claims of Anna Anderson that she was in fact the Grand Duchess Anastasia. I only have one left, from the *Daily Telegraph*, dated 18 February, with the headline: 'ANASTASIA' LOSES HER FIFTY-YEAR FIGHT. Reading the yellow fragment now, I discover that Maria Rasputin—Rasputin's eccentric daughter—was purported to be one of Anna Anderson's supporters. Maria Rasputin later drew attention to herself by claiming, in a book published in 1977, that Rasputin had been raped and castrated by his killers; her co-author claimed to have seen his penis in a velvet case in Paris.

On the back of this one remaining 'Anna Anderson' cutting I can just about decipher forty lines of scrawl listing reasons for the revolution. I seem to have substituted the flourish of foreign words for lucidity and grammar: Lenin plotted '*contra* Nick II' and then '*semper* made trouble for Nick II'. The period after Bloody Sunday (the original, Russian one) is referred to as '*après* BS'. The Bolsheviks and Mensheviks are renamed 'majorytes' and 'minorytes' and Lenin's landlady in London gets a special mention: 'a Mrs Yeo'.

I remember taking my copy of *Nicholas and Alexandra* as a sort of prop when I went to stay with one schoolfriend in Cheshire (very posh, I told my father: 'She says "*fuck awff*"'). On the train journey north we played Botticelli with her mother. I won pointlessly easily

by discreetly scouring the index for obscure Russian names. They usually began with P: Protopopov (the syphilitic minister championed by Alexandra) and Purishkevich (the right-winger who sported a red rose in his fly-buttons).

My interest in the Romanovs did not abate with adulthood. In the Eighties I met an elderly women living in Earls Court who in 1913 had attended the celebrations of 300 years of Romanov rule in St Petersburg. She had actually *seen* the whole family. I remember involuntarily tracing every line on her pretty, pale face. I think I must have hoped to read her memories. Descended from a French family, she spoke English with a French rather than a Russian accent: 'They were wonderfool' is all I can remember her saying. I found an elderly Baroness living in West Kensington who had shaken hands with the Tsar in 1908 in Tallinn. 'What was he like?' I asked in wonder. She shrugged her shoulders: 'What does a little girl know?'

The late Grand Duke Vladimir Romanov, the aspirant Tsar of all the Russias, whom I visited in Brittany, proved the stiffest test of my devotion. In 1991, he was believed to be seriously contemplating a return to the Kremlin. I was cheered, on our initial meeting, by his navy jacket and silver buttons—reminiscent of the jackets worn by Tsar Nicholas and George V in the famous photograph taken at Cowes in 1909. But from the moment we sat down to talk it was clear that he was going to be a disappointment. He seemed notably uncharismatic. His claim that he was like his grandfather, Alexander III, who walked through doors without opening them and tied forks in knots at dinner tables, seemed increasingly absurd. He was currently devoting his life to dealing with a minimal correspondence (ten letters a day). His reticence was, I discovered later, a Romanov trait. Robert K. Massie, in his more recent book, *The Romanovs,* said the family, invariably polylingual, was alluded to as 'silent in six languages'.

The Grand Duke's wife, the Grand Duchess Leonida, was the opposite in every way to the last Tsarina, Alexandra. Where Alexandra was austere, Leonida was radiantly friendly. Where Alexandra was sickly, Leonida was unashamedly robust; where Alexandra occasionally raised her lorgnettes for reading, Leonida was never without her large Dame Edna diamanté glasses. I had not seen photographs of Leonida or her husband before meeting them and I had difficulty believing that this woman was indeed the Grand Duchess. I was convinced I must have misunderstood the Grand Duke until I heard her on the telephone: *'Ici la Grande Duchesse.'*

Why was I so interested in this story? Why did I go on being interested in it? I used to think it had to do with my family history: like something passed on in the genes. Both of my parents had links with pre-revolutionary Russia. My father used to talk about a mysterious trunk owned by my grandmother, full of Russian bonds. My mother's Scottish family lost £30,000 invested in the Putilov steelworks at the time of the Revolution. She made several unsuccessful attempts to trace relevant papers when compensation was offered to the British by Gorbachev in the late Eighties.

Perhaps it was just the story's appeal to nostalgics. Never has a story better encapsulated the tragic end of a golden age. I know I was nostalgic because as a child I dreaded time passing. I had mixed feelings about birthdays; I disliked the passing of ages. When I was ten, I solemnly told a teacher that I had already had the best years of my life—seven till nine. I memorized holiday destinations—the country, town, hotel, even hotel room—because I thought that way I could cheat time. Of course, I remember the name of the cottage— Clematis Cottage—which we were renting when my father first told me about the Romanovs.

Or was it because the story gave flesh and bones to a sorrow that I had sensed but been unable to express or identify? I don't think of my father as sorrowful. But I do feel now that he possessed heightened sensibilities which made him more sad and more joyful than most people. He was melancholy sometimes; he cried when he heard certain music and took no solace from physical comfort. He would have scorned a sofa when he could perch on a wooden stool.

I don't feel qualified to write about him; for one thing he did it so beautifully himself. A journalist, he was deputy editor of the *Daily Telegraph* for sixteen years. He wrote well about his own life: his childhood and the early death of his father; fighting in Normandy in the Second World War. He held conservative views which he said were born of the chaos he saw in Normandy in 1944. It made people like him, he once wrote, 'keenly aware of what had been lost, desperately anxious to preserve what remained'. This conservatism was offset by an eccentric personal life. He travelled on a motorbike in worn leathers, and frequently had too much to drink. My brother once found him slumped over the kitchen table with the cat asleep on his head.

However he was not even predictable in his unpredictability. He combined this image of a Bohemian intellectual with that of a mild country gentleman. He hissed or whistled the same three tunes when he was content, and contentment came to him with physical activity: walking, gardening or cooking. While all his mental activity seemed beset with conundrums, his physical movements were sure. I remember him particularly switching off the gas on my parents' elderly cooker with an elaborate flourish of the wrist.

His champions of pre-revolutionary Russia were predictably controversial. Where everybody else liked Tchaikovsky he favoured Glazunov who, he was fond of relating, sipped vodka through a pipe attached to a barrel under the table. Where everybody else approved of, say, Stolypin, he preferred Goremykin; Goremykin was a president of the Duma who was seventy-seven and in an advanced stage of senility when he was finally removed from office in 1915. 'Goremykin' he would growl at intervals as we attempted to play Trivial Pursuits after a long supper. I savoured any mentions in books of these heroes and was delighted once to find a picture of Goremykin, with curling moustaches cascading down to his chest.

As a child I think I must have sensed that one would have to go to him; you joined him in his world or you didn't join him at all. His affection for his children was unstinting, he would peer dewy-eyed across the table, rub his hands and say 'Derz' fondly. We never found out what he meant. On the other hand he saw no need to back up the affection with concessions. He confronted the vinegar in life's honey and didn't see why his children shouldn't confront it too. My mother knew that I liked eggs and potatoes and was content that I should eat them. My father didn't see why I shouldn't like cabbage and salad. 'You must have the virtue with the vice,' he would say, pieces of cabbage sprouting from his mouth. Once when I came back from boarding school I wept because he had put blue cheese in the mashed potato. My mother understood and was distraught; my father didn't understand but was also distraught.

My mother accepted that I liked the Beatles and even attempted to enjoy one or two songs with me. She gave me *Rubber Soul* for Christmas. My father made diabolical faces and did hideous dances if he came upon me and my brother listening to pop music. He thought I should like classical music and made me listen at least once to *Madame Butterfly* while he told me the story. I stared blankly at the record sleeve. Butterfly received no sympathy from me: imagine loving someone who didn't love you.

I used to ask him endlessly to tell me ghost stories and he would disappoint me by telling me his funny one: a man stays in a haunted house, locks the door, bars the windows and the ghost says, 'Now we're alone together.' Still I pestered and pestered until finally, one evening, he sat me down in a red armchair in the drawing room and read me 'The Old Nurse's Tale' by Mrs Gaskell. I'd asked for terror and that is what I got. I had been a child who liked to walk in the dark, enjoying the sensation of invisibility. 'The Old Nurse's Tale' made me fearful. I came to dread the gathering darkness at the end of each day; in bed I became transfixed by curtains that twitched and open cupboard doors that gaped ominously. Words and phrases I didn't understand—chandeliers, west wing, scar—reverberated in my head. I was convinced that the story's hero, Lord Furnival, lurked behind the large chair in my room. I would run at great speed downstairs. 'I keep on needing to go the loo,' was how I expressed my worries to my mother.

When I was twelve I climbed a mountain in the Cairngorms with my father. I liked being alone with him and the feeling he always imparted of understanding nature. We became thirsty and he said we should swill our mouths out with spring water; we mustn't swallow in case the water was polluted. He made me feel we were not just living, we were surviving. Survival had always appealed to me: as a young child I'd spent a lot of time peering into cupboards, hunting out items that might prove useful in an emergency. As soon as my mother went out to the shops I would rush downstairs and appraise tins in the kitchen cupboards. Who knew what the future had in store?

Much of what my father said I couldn't understand. The fog was between us. I could never understand, for instance, why Beverley Pengelly was *not* a funny name for a schoolgirl where Lettice

Clinkscales was. I remember viewing him as a showman, surrounded by people laughing or gasping with horror. I wanted to watch and enjoy the show but I could never understand what he said. I sometimes think the Romanovs' story was the first story he related which I actually understood. It seemed a simple story, to which it was easy to find the right response. It was as though I touched his hand in the fog.

Then came a shock. When I was sixteen, I discovered something new about my father. My mother told me that he had another family. I had a younger half-brother and half-sister. If he was away, she said, he was probably visiting this other family: he was trying to divide his time between both households. I recall a drawing feeling about my face as the blood left it. I picked at the label on a bottle of wine on the table in front of me and fixed my eyes on the frayed edges. Later, I lay in the bath wondering what sort of reaction one was meant to have after hearing this sort of news. I had at least felt some discomfort downstairs with my mother; alone, I felt nothing. The next time I saw my father, over a Sunday lunch, I tried to look at him in a different way. I wondered if he was looking at me differently, knowing that I knew. Again, the sensation was more in the search for sensation.

Had he tried to talk to me about his situation straight away I think I would have listened. Instead he did not raise the subject until three years later. By this time I did not want to talk to him about it; a sort of portcullis had come down.

He was taking me to Oxford on the back of his motorbike. We were to stay with a friend for Christmas. We stopped at a pub, took off our helmets and ordered food. I was thoroughly enjoying the experience of our being alone together. Over lunch I imagined he might like to hear about my worries and boyfriends. Instead, he began on his own worries. My mouth tightened, I changed colour and looked away. He cursed: 'Oh, for God's sake, let's drop it.' The next time it was mentioned between us was a full ten years later. This time the subject was raised by me. I can't remember why I'd changed my mind about wanting to discuss it; I imagine people had succeeded in convincing me that it was absurd not to talk about it. It was again

Christmas and he was driving me from the station to my parents' house in Wiltshire. We were both looking ahead:

Me: 'I thought it was time we talked…'

My father: 'What about?'

Me: 'You know, about…everything.'

My father: 'Well, what is it you want to know?'

Me: 'I don't know…anything.'

He talked easily and gave me some factual information about my siblings. But the effort of broaching the subject and the relief I felt at its having been broached were so great that I don't remember a single word of what followed.

In our particular father-daughter relationship we weren't able to navel-gaze, discuss affairs of the heart, in the same way I would have done with my mother. Even after I'd met my half-brother and half-sister a few years later, my father and I never went beyond discussing how they were or what they were doing.

It gives me pleasure to throw a particular light back over my childhood, a light able to bring out my father's Russian influence on me. That way I can imagine he planned it all, that the Romanovs were his clever emotional substitute for things too painful for him to talk to me about. Who else in the family, after all, wanted to hear that Nicholas II was in fact very small? ('Not much taller than you.') Of course the idea is preposterous. My father was invariably, as he himself admitted, in a bit of a muddle. He found it difficult enough negotiating his way home every night. However, he did seem to want me to be interested. When I was eight he gave me a record of *Sheherazade*, 'Old Rimsky' being part of the glorious pre-revolutionary old guard. In a rare moment of optimism he must have thought—rightly as it turned out—that I might one day prefer Rimsky-Korsakov to the Beatles.

Later he gave me Galina von Meck's memoirs *As I Remember Them*. His refrain about Galina von Meck was that her father had designed the famously beautiful Moscow Metro stations. Then came two copies—consecutive Christmases—of A. N. Wilson's biography of Tolstoy.

My fascination with the subject remained to him disappointingly lightweight, however. One evening in the House of Commons, where my father was then working as a sketch-writer, we met a mutual

Russian friend who ran the right-wing Association for a Free Russia. I remember my father telling our friend that my interest in the Russians was 'populist'. An intellectual himself, he could never understand why anyone would restrict themselves to the human interest aspect of the story. He would tell me that the Russo-Japanese war in 1905 was in fact a good thing (a controversial opinion). I would politely wait for him to finish, and then report that Alexandra used to force Nicholas to comb his hair with Rasputin's comb before ministerial meetings.

He said I should learn Russian, on the strength of which I signed up for a crash course at the University of East Anglia. But on the rare occasions when I was able to demonstrate my limited knowledge of Russian I felt slightly that the goal posts had been moved and that it hadn't been quite what he was after. I don't know what I expected him to say when I told him I was interviewing the Grand Duke Vladimir. What he did say was that, if I was going via Jersey, I should ring a much-loved soldier friend: 'He'll be in the directory, Plaistow F.' When I reported back that I'd had a very pleasant conversation with Plaistow my father sounded pleased but slightly bemused that I'd rung him.

Yet I know he would not have put down his children intentionally. He would have liked me to have been a nurse; he warned me, after I married, that I mustn't become like Mrs Jellyby (the character in *Bleak House* whose children remain unfed and undressed while she champions the cause of the natives of Borrioboola-Gha). But he enjoyed rubbing his hands and calling me Gloria The Girl Journalist. He read with touching enthusiasm a collection of interviews that I'd recorded with women who'd lived through the Revolution; his copy of the book contains a sheaf of papers covered in his scrawl, presumably raising serious issues unaddressed in the text.

One of my last quests for my father was to find the name of the politician who had compared living under the Tsar in the last days of the monarchy to being driven by a drunken chauffeur: the question was how to wrest control from the driver without killing all the passengers. I finally found the name in Richard Pipes's history of the Revolution. *Maklakov*, I reported back triumphantly on the telephone. My father again sounded bemused, as though he'd forgotten he'd ever wanted to know. 'Who? What?'

My father had a stroke in April 1995 and remained in what is known as a persistent vegetative state until his death almost two years later. During that time, his eyes were open, his facial expressions changed constantly, his limbs moved. Sometimes he would grasp a hand. But nobody knew whether these things meant that he could see or think. He couldn't speak. In the first few months we were told he might be able to see and hear a little. We were told that hearing was always the last sense to go. When I visited I quite often put on the cassette tape of *Sheherazade*. His eyes would open with the first strident blasts from the horn then close with the sweet, falling notes of the violin. In November 1995 I wrote in my diary that I took a copy of *The Fall of the Romanovs* by Mark Steinberg and Vladimir Khrustalev into the hospital, a rehabilitation centre in Bath. The book contained an engaging picture I'd never seen before of the Tsarevich Alexis; he had a bare torso and was standing up in a pond. I held the picture in front of my father's eyes. 'He seemed to try and look at it,' I wrote.

I read him some of the Tsar's diary, extracts of which were included in the book. I first read out the dates, all from July 1918: the month in which the family were shot. I felt that if my father could hear and understand everything, he would understand the significance of the dates. If he could pick up only a few of the words he would find the anodyne nature of the Tsar's diary soothing: '13 July: Alexis took his first bath since Tobolsk; his knee is better, but he can't completely straighten it yet. The weather is warm and pleasant.'

On his seventy-second birthday, 23 April 1996, I took a book about Rasputin to the Savernake hospital, to which my father had moved. I propped up photographs of Rasputin in front of his eyes. I wrote that he seemed to close them upon seeing the pictures. In the first few months nurses would dress him and prop him in a chair. Now he lay in pyjamas under a sheet. After I had held the book up and talked about Rasputin for a while, the nice old man opposite him expressed an interest in seeing the picture. I took it over rather reluctantly. I thought at the time that he must have been very bored to want to talk about Rasputin. I now realize he may have been feeling sorry for me; he might have felt that I needed a response from someone. One of the few comforting aspects of misery is that it can occasionally look worse from the outside.

When my father first had his stroke I became consumed with destiny. I had to pray for him in a church every day. Every other thought was a condition: if the cat walks across the road, he'll be all right, if that women turns and waves, he'll be all right. If the conditions were not met I'd change the conditions. At one point I thought I could bring him back by singing him the tunes he always whistled. One was 'The Birdcatcher's Song' from *The Magic Flute*; the second, which I identified while he was unconscious, was the close of 'The Will-o'-the-Wisp' in Berlioz's *The Damnation of Faust*. The third I have never been able to identify.

For the two years of his unconsciousness my dearest wish was that he would come back. Habitually an insomniac, I found that during this period, perversely, I slept as though I'd been drugged. I relished those rare occasions when I woke in the middle of the night because I could pray for him; I always felt he would slip away when I was off guard.

Looking back, I can see a tiny form of rehearsal for this terror in my reading of the Romanov story. Each time I read the account, I look for loopholes, ways that they might be saved. From the memoirs of Merial Buchanan (the daughter of the British Ambassador in Russia) it appears that the family could have come to England before George V revoked his invitation. New documentation has unearthed the warnings and pleas of a Bolshevik official who was convinced that the family would not survive if they were taken to Yekaterinburg. If only they had stayed in Tobolsk…if only the White army had reached Yekaterinburg a week earlier.

My father stopped breathing at about nine a.m. on 28 January 1997. Now, when he appears in dreams, he is benevolent and indulgent.

Recently I dreamed I saw him taking off his glasses and peering at a book of his collected journalism which we, his family, brought out after his death. 'Super,' he proclaimed with enthusiasm. But I sensed that he only said this to make me feel better. I saw how ridiculous it was ever to have imagined that his feelings for me could have been influenced by my knowledge of the Romanovs, or lack of it. Where he was, nothing mattered except the essentials: whatever made us happy, or, at this point, less unhappy. □

GRANTA

ST NIKOLAI RETURNS
Larry Towell

Under Communism, the annual pilgrimage to return the icon of St Nikolai to the village of Vyelikoryetska, a thousand kilometres north of Moscow, was made in secret. Police would wait to arrest small groups of pilgrims who made the attempt. In its revived form, more than a thousand Orthodox worshippers make the 170 kilometre journey from Kirov cathedral, where the icon is usually kept, to the stump of the tree where, according to tradition, it was found in 1383. Services at the sites of Orthodox churches destroyed under the Soviet regime are held along the route.

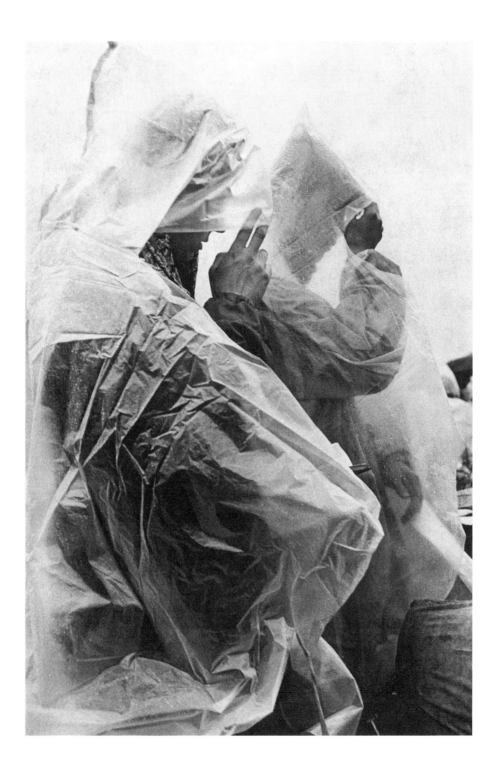

GRANTA

NAPLES IS CLOSED
Barry Unsworth

NOTES FROM ELSEWHERE

Naples had always been high on the list of places I wanted to visit. Ever since coming to live in Italy I had been meaning to spend some time in this city different from any other, so famously beautiful in its setting and violent in its history, so desperately chaotic and vital. But all I had managed was a look at the central railway station while changing trains for Pompeii and a taxi ride to the marvellous museum of Capodimonte on the heights above the city.

Then I found myself writing a novel featuring, indeed centring upon, the life of Horatio Nelson. Impossible to write about Nelson without writing about Naples, where he spent some of the most important—and strangest—months of his life, where he first set eyes on Emma Hamilton, his great love. And of course impossible to write about Naples without first going there. Here was the occasion to combine my long-delayed visit with some pleasurably purposeful authorial research.

The hotel was booked for three days; I couldn't stay longer than this, I had things to do at home. My objectives were carefully planned in advance. I was particularly interested in events between December 1798 and June 1799. During this time Nelson helped the Bourbon ruler of the Two Sicilies, Ferdinand IV, and his Queen, Maria Carolina, to flee from Naples and the advancing French by means of a secret subterranean passage leading from the Royal Palace to the waterside. In the absence of the royal pair the professional and artistic middle class of Naples, together with some of the nobility, fired by republican ideals, rose against the Bourbon tyrant and welcomed the French invader with open arms. With French support they proclaimed a republic, one of the shortest-lived in history, collapsing after five months when the French withdrew and the city was retaken by royalist forces under a warrior-priest named Ruffo. The rebels took refuge from the vengeance of Ferdinand and the fearsome Naples mob who had remained faithful to him in two of the city's forts: the Castel dell'Ovo or Castle of the Egg, so named because legend has it that the castle was built on the exact spot where Virgil had placed an egg, though why he should have done this I couldn't discover; and the Castel Nuovo or New Castle.

Nelson was away at sea when the uprising occurred. Returning to the city in June, he saw the flag of truce flying over the battlements of both the forts and discovered that a treaty had been signed between Ruffo and the rebels, guaranteeing the latter safe conduct either to return to their homes or embark for France if they so chose. Furious at this lenient treatment, Nelson—devoted servant of monarchs—first threatened to break the treaty then appeared to go along with it. The rebels came out of their forts, they were embarked but not allowed to sail, and subsequently handed over to the justice of their king. This was particularly atrocious. Hundreds were put to death in a series of hideous public executions, hundreds more died at the hands of the mob or in the notorious Bourbon jails.

Five places I felt it to be essential I should see: the Royal Palace—if not the escape passage then at least the apartments where Nelson was often entertained; the two forts from which the Neapolitan Jacobins came walking out to their doom; the little church containing the tomb of Caracciolo, the Admiral who joined the rebels and who was tried, condemned and hanged from the yardarm all in one day; and the Piazza Mercato, where the executions were carried out.

Armed with notebook and customary pens—obsessively customary, black for first impressions, red for subsequent insertions—I set off the first morning for the Palazzo Reale. A Tuesday—no good trying to visit anything on a Monday, everything is closed. A half-hour walk from my hotel along the seafront. The great sweep of the bay glittering with sunlight. The pale shape of Capri like the head and muzzle of a swimming animal. Vesuvius mild-looking in the sun, the cindery track of its last eruption clearly visible.

Then across the broad Via Marina and up to the Palace. An enormous, imposing grey and terracotta edifice with a façade that seems as long as a football pitch, lined with statues representing all the dynasties that have lorded it in Naples throughout her troubled history: Hauteville, Hohenstaufen, Angevin, Aragonese, Bourbon. All foreign. Two *carabinieri* in full ceremonial dress, rigidly on guard, flank the real portico of the entrance. Surely not usual at the entrance to a museum? But the huge red and gold banner on the façade over their heads announces the opening hours just as usual. Arrows point across a cobbled courtyard to the ticket office but no ticket office is to be found. Groups of suited men are clustered here and there. I see from the identity cards on their lapels that they are security men. They are not very informative: there is a conference due to be held here, they cannot say if the museum is open to the public. Other would-be visitors are wandering about the courtyard, trying to follow the arrows to the ticket office. Two policemen pass by, very smart in their gleaming white shoulder-straps and revolver-holsters. No, one of them tells me, the museum is not open today. But why? He shrugs and a smile of infinite tolerance and resignation comes to his face. *I ministri*, he says, the ministers. It is explanation enough. Defence, Justice, Foreign Affairs—it makes no difference. For reasons that defy analysis they want to hold a meeting here, they must be humoured. Yes, tomorrow the Palace will be open to the public.

It is now nearly eleven o'clock and not a great deal has yet been achieved in terms of authorial research. A view of the celebrated bay, some minutes of bewilderment, an expression of age-old resignation on a policeman's face. All the same, I feel I need some time to gather myself together again. I find a café with tables on the pavement. More time goes by in the consumption of an espresso than I had really intended because the day is warm and all the life of the city is out on the streets. Neapolitans are intensely communicative people with an inborn sense of theatre and a truly wonderful range of gesture, so there is always much to watch. Just below me, where the street joins the seafront road, *carabinieri* are stopping people on scooters and motorcycles who are not wearing helmets. But the people they stop seem always to be young girls, with whom they laugh and joke at length while hundreds of people, of all ages and both sexes, go whizzing past at dangerous speed and entirely helmetless.

Twenty-five to twelve. Castel Nuovo is just over the way. There would be time to visit it before lunch. An hour would be long enough—it is a question of describing the look of it from outside and getting up to the top so I can look down over the sea-gates the rebels came out from, see the view towards Sorrento as they must have seen it on this last day of their liberty, as they were embarked on the transports that became their floating prisons.

Round, crenellated towers in dark stone, an incongruous white marble triumphal arch celebrating the taking of the city by Alfonso I of Aragon, a wide courtyard, in one corner of which royalist hostages were shot by the panicking rebels in 1799. A flight of stone steps leads upwards. But on the second floor my way is barred by agitated attendants. I hear the slam of heavy doors closing. I must go back down to the courtyard again. What has happened? It can't be closing time, it's not twelve yet. Nobody tells me. There is a good deal of shouting going on among the attendants but the Neapolitan dialect is too difficult, I can't follow it. A different sort of shouting is coming from the street outside, a heavy, reiterated chant. And from some invisible source, high above, other voices, thinned by distance. Finally, back at the ticket office, I am informed of the situation. There is a mass demonstration by the unemployed of Naples—a very numerous class—going on outside. Some of the demonstrators have infiltrated the fort, occupied the battlements—theirs are the thin voices I heard shouting down. These are desperate people, there is fear of some violent assault on the picture gallery, the frescos in the chapel—everything is locked and barred.

A situation like this, once arrived at, can remain unresolved for a very long time in Italy or anywhere else. I suspect that in the end they will have to bring in the riot police. In any case, there doesn't seem much point in hanging about, so I make for the exit gates, only to find these barred too. No one will open the gates for me. Other demonstrators are just outside, they say, waiting for a chance to break in. I am trapped between the occupied battlements and the barred gates. There is a strong element of irony in this; the earnest author, conducting his research into the besieged republicans of 1799, finds himself well and truly besieged in his turn. But I am not really in the right frame of mind to appreciate it. How long is this likely to go on? I ask a morose-looking attendant. He doesn't know. The remote harangues from the men on the battlements still come floating down to us. They may be genuine demonstrators or they may not, the attendant says darkly. Who knows? Naples is reflowering, there will be jobs, but not everybody deserves jobs. This is a new angle on the unemployment problem but I don't ask him what the criteria are. It is clear that among the undeserving are people who occupy the ancient forts of Naples and shout slogans from the battlements.

I pace about for a while. I seem to be alone here. Am I the only visitor or have the others been let out? A woman in a little office just off the courtyard asks me if I am English and appears delighted to learn that I am. Will I check through some tourist information about the fort she has just translated into English? Six pages, closely written, crammed to bursting with mistakes. The translator is pleasant enough but she has no idea of how bad her English is. An hour goes by while I try to correct the text without damaging her self-esteem.

Finally, worn out by this combined linguistic and social strain, I am allowed to leave. No demonstrators in the street outside but about fifty tough-looking police. It is now two p.m. The desire for further research withers in the heat of the Naples afternoon. A pizza and a beer for lunch then back to the hotel for a period of reflection and repose. In the evening, refreshed, I go round the corner of the hotel on to Via Santa Lucia, where stands the small church containing the tomb of Caracciolo. But the gate of the church is padlocked. I ask a nearby shopkeeper the reason for this and learn that the priest died a few days ago. No, there are no immediate plans to reopen the church...

Not much employment for my research pens as yet, either the black one or the red. Day Two is rather cloudy but still warm. My hotel room looks over the little harbour of Santa Lucia, with its white boats and quayside restaurants. I can make out the entrance gate of the other fort, the Castle of the Egg, a little to the north. Above the entrance there is a brightly coloured poster with some words on it, too far away to read, and in the middle what looks like a picture of Donald Duck but of course can't be. This fort is so close, it can be left till later. I decide to make another attempt on the Palazzo Reale. No *carabinieri* on guard this time, which is a good sign, but a deserted air about the place, which is not. I follow the arrows again but again find no ticket office. A passing functionary informs me that the royal apartments are closed to visitors today. Why, is the conference still in process? No, the conference is over but today is Wednesday, the apartments are always closed on Wednesdays.

I am deeply dejected by this news. There is no one to blame but myself. A ministerial conference, the death of a priest, one can be forgiven for not foreseeing these. But this was different, I had failed to check, I had assumed that because throughout Italy museums and public monuments generally close on Mondays, the Royal Palace of Naples would too. Always a fatal mistake to assume uniformity of practice. I walk disconsolately around for a while in the drab, cat-haunted gardens behind the palace. Then in a corner I come upon a piece of statuary in bronze, a group of four people, three men and a woman of varying ages—one is quite old, carrying a scroll, obviously an intellectual. They are supporting one another, heads up, walking forward bravely to confront their fate. Obsessed as I am with the Neapolitan Jacobins of 1799, it seems to me that this might be a group of them walking to the scaffold. Who can I find to ask? Two youngish men are standing together talking, just inside the archway of the rear entrance to the Palace. They have the subtle air of familiarity with the place that employees might have. I approach and ask. They don't know, but a question in Naples always seems to get a full answer, in one way or another. Why don't I go in and ask at the information office? I can visit the reading-rooms of the National Library, second only to that of Florence in size, I can see the painted ceilings and the stucco work, I can see the collection of papyri, unique in Italy. But I thought the Palace was closed to visitors? No, only the royal apartments are closed, all the rest is open.

Borne on the voluble current of their friendliness and civic pride, I find myself mounting the stone steps towards the first-floor office. But it is clearly an information office for students and users of the library, not for people who want to know about statues in the garden. Moreover, it is very crowded. I go on past, up a short flight of stairs, and enter the first of a series of reading-rooms, one leading into another. I have no idea what I am doing here, but the ornate, high-ceilinged rooms and the studious calm of the readers at their long tables make a soothing combination and I wander on. No one asks me my business, no one pays any attention to me. Somehow I take a wrong turning, find myself with bewildering suddenness in a labyrinth of passages, low doorways, twisting flights of steps. Thousands of people lived here in the great days of the Bourbon rulers, now it is occupied with books. I keep coming out on to long galleries filled with volumes, many of them bound in leather, valuable-looking.

I am quite lost by now. I don't think I have ever been alone among so many books before. I have lost all sense of time. I am far away from the Neapolitan Jacobins, far away from Nelson—he wasn't bookish. I am rescued by a man who emerges from among the shelves and advances on me. However, he doesn't demand to know what I am doing there. He asks me, with utmost courtesy, where it is that I would like to go. I have to provide a destination. I remember the words of the men I asked about the statue. The papyrus room, I say, I am trying to find the papyrus room.

He escorts me part of the way, hands me over to a colleague who takes me a little farther, hands me over again—the journey is done in three stages. The papyrus room has big windows, it is full of light. A young woman comes towards me from the desk where she has been working. She does not ask me who I am or what is the purpose of my visit. She smiles as if she is glad to see me and begins immediately to tell me about the papyri. She shows me the scrolls as they are first found, coal-black, amorphous, completely carbonized. They are all from Herculaneum. It is a fascinating story. Herculaneum is farther from Vesuvius than Pompeii, so the eruption of AD 79 did not cover it with lava but with a heavy layer of ash. Below this layer the papyrus scrolls were carbonized and so preserved. Then, in the 1750s, there began the laborious process of retrieving and deciphering them, which still continues today. The librarian explains how this is done: a special preparation of gelatine is used to soften the strips, then there is the gradual unfolding and photographing, then the printing in volume form—she shows me a page, original Greek on one side, Latin translation on the other. Work requiring enormous patience—a single scroll can take a year. She shows almost as much patience with me, sacrificing half an hour of her time to explain these things.

I thank her and am conducted back to the information office, which is even more crowded than before. It is lunchtime, I am hungry, I decide not to wait. I return to Santa Lucia, find a restaurant beside the water, have *calamari fritti* and a half-litre of Ischian white wine. By the time this is consumed, the research impulse has lost something of its élan. Besides, everything is closing for the afternoon. I linger over the coffee. Never have I seen so many people with mobile phones. They walk along beside the water, talking loudly into their phones and gesticulating. They stand in groups, conversing with one another and with their phones at the same time and at the same volume. There are more people living on the breadline here than almost anywhere else in Europe. There are chronically high levels of unemployment. But for a people so intensely communicative a mobile phone seems to be worth making sacrifices for.

In the early evening I make my way to the Castle of the Egg, so conveniently close to my hotel. I shall finally be able to get that sense of atmosphere I feel I need, see things as the rebels saw them that bright morning 200 years ago when they came out of their forts... The figure on the poster over the entrance, which I had not believed could be Donald Duck, in fact turns out to be him after all. I can read the words now: UN MONDO DI PAPERI, The World of Donald Duck. After a brief interlude of incredulity I realize that a Donald Duck exhibition is being held inside this ancient and venerable building. Perhaps I can bypass Donald, get a ticket for the fort only. But no, it is a combined ticket, you can't have one without the other. Perhaps then I can avoid going in, ignore Donald altogether. It is not that I have anything against him but he doesn't really fit in with my research plans. I will walk past, make my way up to the sunlit bastions, inspect the rusty cannons...

But at the entrance to the exhibition there are two young people, a boy and a girl, they are wearing Donald Duck T-shirts, they smile in greeting, they have seen the brightly coloured ticket in my hand, it too bearing Donald's image, they think I have come for him. I have always found it difficult to disappoint people, especially when the people are young and smiling in welcome and wearing ridiculous T-shirts. I hastily assume the expression of a man looking forward to total immersion in Donald Duck and turn into the exhibition. Once in, there is no quick way out and no retreat. It is a one-way system, arrows point from room to room. The exhibition is enormous, it occupies three floors. All Donald's relatives are hugely featured on the walls, together with large-scale extracts from their amazing adventures. The Scottish branch is well represented, Jack McDuck and Dirty Dingus and Sir Quackly; and all the cousins are there— Cuthbert Coot, Molly Mallard, Luke Goose. Mounting higher, room by room, I peer from the slits of windows at the brilliant sea, the broken crest of Vesuvius, the mole of the fort directly below me, along which the Jacobins made their way to be embarked. This is the view I wanted. Turning back I encounter the baleful gaze of old Scrooge McDuck or a boatload of jowly dog-pirates in black masks. I am forming a set of associations here which have little to do with the scheme of my novel.

All the same it is a wonderful show in its way. The primary colours shriek from the walls. The graphics are superb. And in one corner of a room on the third and final floor, I find at least the encouragement of symbol. Here some famous paintings have been reproduced by Italian artists, faithful in every particular except that the human subjects have been replaced by Disney characters. There is the Arnolfini Marriage by Jan van Eyck, with the Happy Hippos, Horace and Clarabella, as the engaged couple. There is Caravaggio's celebrated *Lute Player*, with Minnie Mouse playing the lute. This is what, in a way, I hope to do in my novel: interfuse the present and the past so that both can be looked at differently.

Only one morning left now. I have to be back in Rome by early evening. I am at the Palazzo Reale bright and early—no trouble getting in this time. A total anticlimax, however—the apartments of former royal palaces converted to museums are pretty much the same anywhere, I should have known that. Damask and gilt, roped-off bedchambers, stately ante-rooms, silk tapestries—I could have got it all from a good guidebook. I leave in a hurry, forgetting to ask about the bronze figures in the garden. There is just time to see Piazza Mercato, for centuries the place of public execution in Naples. Here in 1269, Conradin, last of the Hohenstaufen princes, was beheaded and the Angevins took over the city. Here the Neapolitan Jacobins were brought to be hanged before a jubilant mob.

A large and desolate square between the dock area and the district of Forcella, where the main Camorra families traditionally live. A few nondescript stalls. Along the eastern side an open-air market for cheap beach-goods, brightly coloured plastic chairs, inflatable rubber swimming pools, umbrellas, all set out on the dark cobbles. Some small boys kicking a ball about. A baroque church with a lead-coloured dome and eroded prelates on the façade. That huge sum of agony—one would somehow expect to find it reflected here; but there is only the bleakness and ugliness of the present.

Of course, I have to go back. ☐

NOTES ON CONTRIBUTORS

Heidi Bradner has been photographing in the former Soviet Union since 1992. She was awarded the Leica Medal of Excellence for Documentary Photography in 1997.

Robert and **Elizabeth Chandler** and **Angela Livingstone** are the co-translators of *The Return*, a selection of Andrei Platonov's stories to be published by Harvill in spring 1999.

Orlando Figes teaches at Trinity College, Cambridge. His history of the Russian Revolution, *A People's Tragedy*, is published by Jonathan Cape in Britain and Viking Penguin in the US. His next book, on Russia's cultural golden age, will be published by Granta Books.

Masha Gessen is a journalist in Moscow. Her study of the Russian intelligentsia after Communism, *Dead Again*, is published by Verso.

Charlotte Hobson studied Russian in Voronezh. She has recently translated *The Three Sisters* for the Oxford Stage Company.

Angus Macqueen is a documentary film maker who specializes in the Soviet Union and Eastern Europe, mainly for the BBC.

Victor Pelevin's novel *Omon Ra* was published by Faber in Britain and Farrar, Straus and Giroux in the US in 1996. 'Moscow Dynamo' is taken from his new novel, *The Clay Machine-Gun*, which will be published jointly by Faber and Harbord in 1999.

Anna Pyasetskaya is the founder of a joint Chechen-Russian organization which counsels and represents people still searching for missing family members. 'The Lost Boys' was first published in *Karta*, a Russian journal dedicated to human-rights issues.

John Ranard has been sponsored by the Open Society Institute/ The Lindesmith Center to photograph the relationship between drug culture and HIV in the Russian Federation.

Colin Thubron explored western Russia in the late Brezhnev years for *Among the Russians*, 1983. His last novel, *Distance*, was published in 1996 by Heinemann. He is working on a book about Siberia.

Larry Towell has been a Magnum photographer since 1989. His most recent book, *Then Palestine*, has just been published by Aperture.

Barry Unsworth's latest novel, *Morality Play*, is published by Hamish Hamilton in Britain and Nan A. Talese in the US. His previous novel, *Sacred Hunger*, was joint winner of the 1992 Booker Prize.

Vitali Vitaliev left Moscow for the West in 1990. His latest book, *Borders Up: Eastern Europe Through the Bottom of a Glass,* will be published by Simon and Schuster in April 1999.

Frances Welch is the co-author of *Memories of Revolution* which was published by Routledge in 1993. She writes for the *Sunday Telegraph*.